My Bad

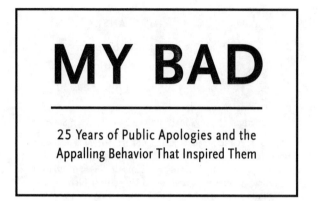

MY BAD

25 Years of Public Apologies and the
Appalling Behavior That Inspired Them

PAUL SLANSKY
and
ARLEEN SORKIN

BLOOMSBURY

Published by Bloomsbury Publishing, New York and London
Distributed to the trade by Holtzbrinck Publishers

All papers used by Bloomsbury Publishing are natural, recyclable products made from wood grown in well-managed forests. The manufacturing processes conform to the environmental regulations of the country of origin.

LIBRARY OF CONGRESS CATALOGING-IN-PUBLICATION DATA

My bad : 25 years of public apologies and the appalling behavior that inspired them / [edited by] Paul Slansky and Arlene Sorkin.—
1st U.S. ed.
p. cm.
Includes index.
ISBN-13: 978-1-58234-521-5
ISBN-10: 1-58234-521-X
1. Apologies. I. Slansky, Paul. II. Sorkin, Arleen.
PN6278.4.M9 2006
081—dc22
2005030618

First U.S. Edition 2006

1 3 5 7 9 10 8 6 4 2

Typeset by Palimpsest Book Production Limited,
Polmont, Stirlingshire, Scotland
Printed in the United States of America by
Quebecor World Fairfield

For everyone either of us has ever wronged

Contents

Introduction

To err is human, to err in public humiliating.

Or so you would think. There was a time, after all, when bad behavior was judged harshly, when transgressors had the decency to be properly embarrassed, and when redemption had to be sorely earned.

Not anymore. Over the past quarter century, the public apology—offered up in tones ranging from grudging to groveling by the famous and the infamous as they seek understanding and absolution for offenses intended and inadvertent—has come to provide forgiveness for its author without the discomfort of disgrace. It's like going bankrupt and getting to keep your credit cards.

There's a classic *Peanuts* comic strip in which Lucy goes around asking everyone to sign a piece of paper. "Just sign it . . . that's right . . . thank you," she says. "No matter what happens any place or any time in the world, this absolves me from all blame!" To which Charlie Brown observes, "That must be a nice document to have."

The public apology has become the equivalent of Lucy's document. Any misdeed, no matter how egregious, can now be immediately negated by a bleat of casual contrition. Got a crack habit? Oops, sorry. Blurted out an ethnic slur? Didn't mean it. Caught with a woman not your wife? My bad.

That these expressions of regret are usually more expedient than heartfelt should, of course, render them meaningless, but the persistent decline in standards in the conduct of public affairs has significantly lowered the bar for forgiveness. Kids are taught by parents that apologies have to be genuine to be accepted—"Don't just say it because you got caught, say it because you mean it"—but today's society sends a different message: going through the motions is enough.

To be sure, public apologies go back at least as far as Plato. What's different here is the sheer volume of wrongdoers rushing forward to get their repentance on record and the culture's willingness to grant them speedy pardons despite the obvious lack of sincerity that imbues most of their efforts. "In our age of instant remorse," wrote historian Tony Judt in the *Washington Post*, "the currency of penitence has been hyperinflated and has lost almost all its value."

One factor contributing to the current apology glut is the advent of political correctness, which, while making it no longer okay to say one doesn't like black people (or gay people, or poor people, or Jews, or whomever), fails to keep a lot of people from saying precisely such things anyway, and then demands that they feign sorrow. The patently bogus retractions that follow are by definition inadequate, because what they're basically saying is "I'm sorry I was unable to keep my true awfulness hidden." And we're all sorry we had to see it, but you know, whatever.

At the same time, the news media have moved away from the kind of solid reporting that just a few decades ago brought down a president, and toward the no-heavy-lifting "gotcha" journalism that turns reporters into hall monitors waiting to pounce, relentlessly serving up the faux pas and foibles of the famous for public consumption. Between the twenty-four-hour news channels and the Internet there's a lot of space to be filled with lots of things, among them this mandatory rite of passage for sinners who wish to rejoin polite society.

Add to all this the lack of shame that increasingly defines our national discourse, and the absence of real consequence for doing or saying pretty much anything, and it's small wonder that little time passes between fresh mea culpas. The genre even has its own chronicler in satirist Harry Shearer, who since November 2001 has been presenting the Apologies of the Week on his radio hour, *Le Show*.

While it has truly flowered over the past twenty-five years, the Apology Era took root a half century ago with the spectacle of Richard Nixon's 1952 "Checkers speech," so named for its mawkish references to the cocker spaniel that someone had given his two young daughters. Dwight Eisenhower's vice presidential nominee, faced with a blooming scandal over an eighteen-thousand-dollar slush fund, saved his place on the Republican ticket by going on live TV to defend himself against charges of financial improprieties. The half-hour speech contained not a single syllable of regret, with Nixon contenting himself to wallow in the muck of self-pity as, with his mortified wife looking on, he bared his family's financial history right down to the gratuitous revelation that "Pat doesn't have a mink coat." The success of this approach sent out the depressing message that shame was going to become not just expendable in public life but actually counterproductive.

Ironically, Nixon's personal inability to apologize may well have helped popularize apologies. Had he preempted the Watergate scandal in 1972 by tossing off an "I'm sorry" in the giddy wake of his forty-nine-state reelection landslide, he would never have had to resign in 1974, and the country that was dealing with three assassinations and losing its first war wouldn't have also had to deal with the fact that it had elected a criminal president. That country might very well not have gone quite so crazy as it did, and the whole notion of people being able to get away with *anything* as long as they then spoke words of remorse might never have taken hold. (Certainly if Nixon had his way, it wouldn't have. He shared his position on contrition with interviewer David Frost in 1977: "If they want me to get down and grovel on the floor, no. Never.")

Have we mentioned Nixon? He also gave us the prototypes for modern-day apologists with his vice president, Spiro Agnew (whose first burst of fame was for referring to a reporter as a "fat Jap"), and his agriculture secretary, Earl Butz, who self-immolated in 1976 when he told a racist joke of breathtaking grossness within earshot of a reporter. Butz's subsequent apology failed in its main purpose, which was to save his job. But it provided a template for the responsibility-fudging ("I regret any offense which may have been given to any person or to any group"), blame-shifting ("I was merely repeating a comment made decades ago by a ward politician in a large Midwestern city"), and self-flagellation with a feather ("even that is no excuse for the incident") that define the hollow, squirm-inducing pleas with which quasi-penitent misbehavers have been bombarding us for too many years.

The truth is that the format has become predictable. Not only is there no suspense about *if* an offense will be followed by an apology, but even the *when* has become humdrum. We suggest giving it back some heat by reintroducing the humiliation that used to provide the penance part of the whole moral exchange. Imagine a reality show called *Who's Sorry Now*, with a panel of judges confronting the week's apologists like misbehaving children, and telling them, like their parents should have, "Don't just say it because you got caught. *Convince us that you mean it.*" Who wouldn't watch that show?

Meanwhile, enjoy the brazen displays of bigotry, vulgarity, criminality, and just plain idiocy atoned for herein, and marvel at the bizarre cleansing ritual that these sorry times have created.

Media Mea Culpas

"I need to make quick clarification and apology for something, an offhand, flippant comment that slipped out on the air as, not certainly as it was intended. You may have heard it earlier, a comment not intended for air. It was errantly recorded and transmitted unbeknownst to us here in the KSC newsroom. Please rest assured that I have the highest respect for the first lady and her role and am very pleased to see that Mrs. Clinton saw this launch as important enough to make a return visit."

Steve Rondinaro, news anchor on WFTV in Orlando, apologizing for his comments regarding Hillary Clinton's arrival at Florida's Kennedy Space Center for a shuttle launch: "Just moments ago the First Lady rolled in. There she comes, the old battle-ax. There she is with Chelsea in tow."
July 21, 1999

"As much of the English-speaking world knows by now, the *Post* reported on yesterday's front page that John Kerry had chosen Dick Gephardt to be his running mate. Obviously, we were wrong—and we'd like to humbly apologize to our readers for the mistake . . . Rest assured that generous helpings of crow were eaten here yesterday—and the leftovers will surely last a few more days . . . We do hope you'll forgive the error—it certainly was one for the record books."

The *New York Post*, apologizing under the headline WE GOT IT WRONG. *July 7, 2004*

====

"CBS News regrets, as does Mike Wallace, his off-hand remark during a break in an interview. The story, as it was broadcast on *60 Minutes*, was accurate and fair and in no way reflected that remark."

CBS News apologizing for an exchange, captured on tape, in which savings and loan officers acknowledged that the contracts they gave customers were hard to read, to which Mike Wallace—unaware that the cameras were still rolling—replied, "You bet your ass they're hard to read if you're reading them over the watermelon or over the tacos." *January 26, 1982*

====

"I apologize for my conduct and I'm sorry I did it."

Robert Novak apologizing for overreacting to his CNN colleague James Carville's on-air teasing in the wake of his involvement in the outing of CIA agent Valerie Plame by saying, "Well, I think that's bullshit" and walking off the set. Said CNN, "We've asked him to take some time off." *August 5, 2005*

====

"If committing mass suicide would help, I've even given that some consideration. Nothing has upset me more probably in my whole life . . . I'll take my shirt off and beat myself

bloody on the back . . . I couldn't hurt any more if I was bleeding."

CNN founder Ted Turner apologizing for the network's inaccuracy-riddled Operation Tailwind report claiming that, in 1970, U.S. troops used nerve gas in Laos in an effort to kill American defectors. "This is a big blow. This one really hurts . . . a major, self-inflicted wound," said CNN News Group chairman Tom Johnson. "There is insufficient evidence that sarin or any other deadly gas was used . . . We apologize to our viewers and to our colleagues at *Time* [which, thanks to the wonders of corporate synergy, was the print partner for the story] for this mistake." Retired Maj. Gen. Perry Smith, CNN's military expert, resigned in protest after the report aired, calling it "as bad a piece of television journalism as I can ever remember. I can't think of anything worse." *July 10, 1998*

"I made some comments that seemed to stereotype women in an exceptionally unfortunate way. The plain fact is, I misspoke. And for this I feel doubly badly and extend my profound apologies to anyone whom I offended."

Los Angeles Times publisher Mark H. Willes apologizing for suggesting that more women would read the paper if it ran stories that were less analytical and more emotional. *June 1, 1998*

"I apologize if any harm has been done. The story was issued in good faith. It was based on two sources who clearly were operating from a political motivation."

Matt Drudge apologizing to White House aide Sidney Blumenthal and retracting a story on his Drudge Report Web site alleging that Blumenthal "has a spousal abuse past that has been effectively covered up." Said William McDaniel, Blumenthal's attorney, "The Blumenthals are not going to stand for this . . . We don't want a retraction. This is drivel. This is garbage. We intend to prove there isn't a shred of truth in that report . . . He made this up. If he's got sources, they made it up." *August 11, 1997*

⸻

"First, it should be said (I wish it went without saying) that no racial implication was intended, by *Time* or by the artist. One could argue that it is racist to say that blacker is more sinister . . . but that does not excuse insensitivity. To the extent that this caused offense to anyone, I deeply regret it."

Time managing editor James R. Gaines in a letter to readers apologizing for darkening O. J. Simpson's skin in the mug shot that appeared on the magazine's cover. *June 27, 1994*

⸻

"This is, again, an embarrassment not only to the governor but to the *Globe*. We apologize to Governor Dukakis a second time. We are now investigating how it happened and should we discover the person or persons responsible, immediate dismissal will be in order."

Boston Globe spokesman Richard Gulla apologizing for his paper's running, for the second time, a photograph of Michael Dukakis in which a mustache had been scratched onto the printing plate. *January 13, 1988*

===

"We regret the insensitive tone of the statement and apologize to anyone who was offended by it."

Joe Angio, editor of *Time Out New York*, apologizing for his magazine's description of recently deceased Cardinal John O'Connor as a "pious creep [who] was a stuck-in-the-1950s anti-gay menace. Good riddance!" *January 4, 2001*

===

"All we have in this business is our credibility—your trust that we get it right. I will make every effort to see that it never happens again."

Antienvironmental crusader John Stossel, the Bizarro World version of a young Ralph Nader, apologizing under orders of ABC News for rebroadcasting a controversial *20/20* report pooh-poohing the notion that organic food was any safer than regular food—and implying that it was *maybe even more dangerous!* It turned out that the test that was the basis for his claim that there was no pesticide residue on nonorganic food was never actually performed. *August 11, 2000*

===

"'Jimmy's World' was in essence a fabrication. I never encountered or interviewed an 8-year-old heroin addict. The September 28, 1980, article in *The Washington Post* was a serious misrepresentation which I deeply regret. I apologize to my newspaper, my profession, the Pulitzer board and all seekers of the truth. Today, in facing up to the truth, I have submitted my resignation."

Washington Post reporter Janet Cooke apologizing in a statement written in longhand after admitting that her Pulitzer
Prize–winning story was largely made up. Discrepancies in
the autobiography submitted by Cooke to the Pulitzer
board—specifically, unearned college degrees and unverifi-
able professional accomplishments—set the unraveling in
motion. *April 15, 1981*

—

**"We apologize. This newspaper . . . was itself the victim of a
hoax—which we then passed along in a prominent page-one
story, taking in the readers as we ourselves had been taken
in . . . The sheer magnitude and breathtaking gall of the
deception—its size—made it harder to detect . . . The rock-
bottom element of trust and the assumption of good faith
that must exist in any professional relationship diminish the
chances that you will spot a huge scam right away. You just
do not read a many-paged memorandum from an apparently reliable reporter, relating her visit to and prolonged
conversation with several people in great detail, and then
inquire: 'Say, did any of this actually happen?' . . . You may
be plenty sure that there will be lots of self-examination . . .
on our own interior workings. One of these episodes is one
too many."**

The *Washington Post* apologizing in an editorial for having
run Janet Cooke's story. *April 16, 1981*

—

**"We offer no excuses for any of this. Only our deepest
apologies to all concerned."**

The *New Republic* apologizing for running twenty-seven

articles by reporter/fantasist Stephen Glass that contained at least some fabricated elements, six of which "could be considered entirely or nearly entirely made up." *June 11, 1998*

———

"I remain truly sorry for my lapses in journalistic integrity. I continue to struggle with recurring issues that have caused me great pain."

Former *New York Times* reporter Jayson Blair apologizing in a statement to the Associated Press for turning out thirty-six plagiarized and/or fabricated stories for the paper, often with datelines from locations he didn't even travel to. Though the paper's metropolitan editor, Jonathan Landman, had earlier warned that Blair's "unprofessional" behavior warranted his being fired, his being black was widely believed to be a factor in the way his case was handled, and he was promoted to the national desk without his new editors being warned about potential trouble. His two biggest champions at the paper— executive editor Howell Raines and managing editor Gerald Boyd—resigned as a result of the scandal. *May 13, 2003*

———

"I recognize that I cannot make amends for the harm I have caused to my family, friends and colleagues. Nor can I make it up to readers who depend upon good journalism to understand a chaotic and confusing world. I can only offer my sincere apology to those I have let down. Although I remain proud of much of the work I did over twenty-one years, I understand that what I did wrong will diminish what I did right."

Resigned *USA Today* reporter Jack Kelley—who once said he

became a newspaperman because "God has called me to proclaim truth"—apologizing for "a number of serious mistakes that violate the values that are most important to me as a person and as a journalist." *April 21, 2004*

—

"Joe Bob Briggs' column that appeared in Friday's *Times Herald* offended many readers. The *Times Herald* deeply regrets that the column was published. It was a misdirected attempt at satire. A great deal of insensitivity was reflected in the column. We apologize."

The *Dallas Times Herald* apologizing on its front page for running a parody of the song "We Are the World" with lyrics that included "There are Negroes dying / And it's time to make 'em eat" and the chorus, "We are the weird/We are the starvin'/We are the scum of the filthy earth/So let's start scarfin'." The paper permanently dropped the weekly "Joe Bob Goes to the Drive-in" feature—in which columnist John Bloom satirically assumed the persona of an ignorant redneck—because it was too often "misunderstood." *April 16, 1985*

—

"We're apologizing for the headline, but it was written before her death."

Globe editorial director Dan Schwartz apologizing for the tabloid's Princess Diana headline in the issue on sale the week after her death: TO DI FOR. *September 2, 1997*

—

"We feel terrible about this. It was a mistake on the editors' part, which won't happen again."

American Media spokesman Stuart Zakim apologizing for a "Top 10 Ugliest People" feature in the tabloid *Weekly World News* that included a photo of a Phoenix, AZ, cop whose unattractiveness was the result of a car accident that left his face hideously burned. *February 3, 2005*

——

"A two-sentence blind item we ran here on Dec. 19 about a 'Hall of Fame baseball hero' has sparked a series of unfortunate consequences for which we are very sorry."

The *New York Post* apologizing for a Page Six gossip item implying that former Dodgers pitcher Sandy Koufax is gay— an apology tendered only after Koufax informed the Dodgers that, because of the item in the Murdoch-owned paper, he was severing all ties to the then-Murdoch-owned team. *February 21, 2003*

——

"It was a serious mistake, which I acknowledge. No one believes more strongly in CBS News standards than I do, and I have let those standards down."

CBS News anchor Dan Rather apologizing for the "embarrassing and regrettable error in judgment" he made by speaking at a Democratic fund-raiser in Austin. Rather claimed that he didn't know the event was a fund-raiser until he arrived there, prompting Texas Republican Party chair Susan Weddington to say, "This is a newsman. If he didn't know before he hit Texas that this was a fund-raiser of which his daughter was a sponsor, perhaps the network should reevaluate his competence to deliver the news." *April 4, 2001*

——

"I didn't intend the column to sound the way it turned out. Unfortunately, the need to babble as often as I do sometimes leads to unintended and unfortunate results. To those who were offended—readers and colleagues—I apologize."

The *Chicago Tribune*'s Mike Royko apologizing for a column in which he complained about African American parents who give their kids unusual names. *January 22, 1996*

—

"To the people I work with. I am no good and once again I can prove it . . . I am sorry. I said things I shouldn't have said. The racial and sexual insults I spewed are never appropriate."

New York Newsday columnist Jimmy Breslin apologizing in an e-mail message to fellow staffers for a profane newsroom rant in which he referred to reporter Ji-Yeon Mary Yuh as "a yellow cur" and "slant-eyed" after she sent him an e-mail message criticizing the sexism in a piece he'd written. *May 4, 1990*

—

"I should not have used a slang term for Polish. It was poor judgment, and I apologize."

Advice columnist Ann Landers apologizing for calling Pope John Paul II "a Polack." *November 30, 1995*

—

"Earlier Friday, FOXNews.com posted an item purporting to contain quotations from Kerry. The item was based on a reporter's partial script that had been written in jest and should not have been posted or broadcast. We regret the error, which occurred because of fatigue and bad judgment, not malice."

Fox News apologizing for a story on its Web site after the first Kerry-Bush debate in which John Kerry was quoted as saying, "Women should like me! I do manicures" and "Didn't my nails and cuticles look great? What a good debate!" and defining his differences with Bush as "I'm metrosexual—he's a cowboy!" *October 1, 2004*

—

"We deeply regret we included the inappropriate demonstration in our *Dateline* report. We apologize to our viewers and to General Motors. We have also concluded that unscientific demonstrations should have no place in hard news stories at NBC. That's our new policy."

Dateline NBC anchors Stone Phillips and Jane Pauley apologizing for a report about the proclivity of General Motors trucks to burst into flames when struck from the side. It turned out that the fireball that ignited during a thirty-miles-per-hour demonstration crash was enhanced by toy-rocket motors that had been placed under the truck and set off by remote control. "We agree with GM that we should have told our viewers about these devices," Pauley said. "We acknowledge the placing of the incendiary devices under the truck was a bad idea from start to finish." *February 9, 1993*

—

"We regret the inappropriate video to illustrate what was otherwise an accurate report."

NBC News anchor Tom Brokaw apologizing for the use of footage of dead fish "from another forest further south, not from Clearwater" in a report on endangered fish in Idaho's Clearwater National Forest. Brokaw also set the record straight about other footage used in the story in which fish appeared to be dead. "In fact, they were not," he said. "They had been stunned for testing purposes." *February 24, 1993*

===

"Just one other note about the Bloch case, which was first revealed on this broadcast last Friday. In that first report, we simulated a transaction which our intelligence sources told us had taken place between Bloch and a known Soviet agent. We did not label that simulation as clearly or as quickly as we should have. It was a production error. We're sorry if anyone was misled and we will try to see that it doesn't happen again."

ABC News anchor Peter Jennings apologizing for airing footage of an unlabeled reenactment of American diplomat Felix Bloch handing a briefcase to a Soviet agent. *July 25, 1989*

===

"We, you, and television viewers in fourteen other countries were taken. To make amends, we felt obligated to lay it all out in detail and ask you to please accept our apology."

60 Minutes executive producer Don Hewitt appearing on camera for the first time in the show's then-thirty-year history to apologize for airing a story about heroin smuggling based on a British documentary that turned out to have been largely faked. *December 13, 1998*

===

"We made a mistake in judgment, and for that I am sorry. It was an error that was made, however, in good faith and in the spirit of trying to carry on a CBS News tradition of investigative reporting without fear or favoritism."

CBS News anchor Dan Rather apologizing for blowing the *60 Minutes II* story about George W. Bush's questionable service in the Texas National Guard by relying on documents whose authenticity could not be verified (and may well have been part of a setup by the Bush campaign), thus allowing the rest of the mainstream media to dismiss as without merit the entire question of whether Bush received favorable treatment despite failing to fulfill his duties. *September 20, 2004*

"It has come to the editor's attention that the *Herald-Leader* neglected to cover the civil rights movement. We regret the omission."

The *Lexington (KY) Herald-Leader* apologizing for the forty-year-old policies of the then-separate papers the *Herald* and the *Leader* to relegate coverage of sit-ins, marches, and the like to brief mentions in a column called "Colored Notes." *July 4, 2004*

"I wish to retract the item that appeared in the *Washington Post* concerning reports that Blair House was 'bugged' during President-elect Reagan's stay there. I also wish to apologize to both of you for its publication and regret any embarrassment that it caused you . . . When we published the item we had a source whom we believed to be credible and reliable, and he identified his sources as two members of your family . . . We now believe the story he told us to have been wrong and that there was no 'bugging' of Blair House during your administration. Nor do we now believe that members of your family said Blair House was 'bugged.'"

Washington Post publisher Donald E. Graham apologizing in a letter to former president Jimmy Carter and his wife, Rosalynn, who had been threatening to file a seven-figure libel lawsuit over an item in the paper's October 5 Ear column that claimed the Carters had bugged the Reagans during one of their preinaugural stays. According to the gossip column, the bug was the source of a December 1980 UPI report that Nancy Reagan wanted the Carters to move out early so she could get started on her redecorating. *October 22, 1981*

———

"We have expressed to Mr. Cooke our concern that anything we have published should have caused him embarrassment or pain. We acknowledge that the inclusion of material in the article that suggested to anyone that he had any participation in, or knowledge of, game-fixing, that he ever condoned or practiced racism or political corruption was a lapse in editorial judgment."

The *Washingtonian* apologizing to Washington Redskins owner Jack Kent Cooke in what turned out to be merely the first of three major-lawsuit-avoiding apologies (the others were to Gerald Ford's former press secretary Ron Nessen and People for the Ethical Treatment of Animals) published by the magazine in the space of just a few months. *August 8, 1991*

———

"I'm sorry that it happened and I assure you that it was inadvertent. Nobody was hurt by what I said. No mission was compromised . . . I should have been more careful."

Fox News correspondent Geraldo Rivera apologizing for getting himself kicked out of Iraq after diagramming planned U.S. troop movements in the sand for viewers. Before apologizing, he'd denied his ouster as "a pack of lies" being spread by "some rats" at his former network (NBC) who "can't compete fair and square on the battlefield, so they're trying to stab me in the back." *April 6, 2003*

━━

"Trudeau takes full responsibility, acknowledging the use of fictional material from an outside source instead of simply making it up as he usually does. The creator deeply apologizes for unsettling anyone who was under the impression that the president is, in fact, quite intelligent."

The *Doonesbury* Web site "apologizing" for creator Garry Trudeau's having been fooled by, and incorporating into his comic strip, an Internet hoax claiming that a research study conducted by a nonexistent institute found George W. Bush to have the lowest IQ of any White House occupant in the past half century. *September 5, 2001*

━━

"*Time* maintains strict procedures for acceptance of advertising materials, but, regrettably, our system failed to prevent the appearance of the advertisement. We apologize for the lapse."

Time magazine apologizing for an ad in its UK edition that used the slogan "Poor use of color can ruin your presentation" with the image of faded red swastikas. *May 31, 1989*

———

"Accusing a Christian of adoring money above all else does not engage any history of ugly stereotypes. Accuse a Jewish person of this and you invoke a thousand years of stereotypes about that which Jews have specific historical reasons to fear. What I wrote here was simply wrong, and for being wrong, I apologize."

Gregg Easterbrook apologizing for a blog entry on the *New Republic*'s Web site in which he attacked the violence in the Quentin Tarantino film *Kill Bill* and referred to Disney CEO Michael Eisner and Miramax head Harvey Weinstein as "Jewish executives" who "worship money above all else." *October 16, 2003*

———

"I'm reminded of something I wrote years ago. 'It may be impossible to be objective,' I said, 'but we must always be fair.' Well, after a long Election Day and seven hours on the set, what I said on the Election Night coverage was both impolite and unfair. I'm sorry. I regret it."

ABC's David Brinkley beginning the final broadcast of *This Week with David Brinkley* by apologizing to President Bill Clinton (his final guest) for his closing comment on Election Night: "Bill Clinton . . . has not a creative bone in his body. Therefore, he's a bore and will always be a bore." Clinton graciously accepted the apology, saying, "I always believe you have to judge people on their whole work and if you get judged based on your whole work, you come out way ahead." *November 10, 1996*

===

"You can't write that something happened that didn't, even if it's just who sat in the stands. We—the editors and I—got caught in an assumption that shouldn't have happened. It won't again."

Detroit Free Press sportswriter Mitch Albom apologizing for a column written a day before a Final Four basketball game (but in the past tense, as if it was written after the game) in which, based on their stated intentions to him, he reported that two former Michigan State players "sat in the stands, in their MSU clothing, and rooted on their alma mater" as their team lost to North Carolina. Unfortunately, something came up and they didn't actually attend the game. *April 7, 2005*

===

"We regret that we got any part of our story wrong, and extend our sympathies to victims of the violence and to the U.S. soldiers caught in its midst."

Mark Whitaker, editor of *Newsweek*, apologizing in a note to readers for his magazine's erroneous allegation that U.S. interrogators at Guantanamo Bay tried to get Muslim detainees to talk by flushing a copy of the Koran down the toilet—a report that ignited rioting in Muslim countries that led to at least fifteen deaths. White House spin led the media to act as if the big story here was *Newsweek*'s error, obscuring the fact that other disrespectful acts toward the prisoners' Korans—including kicking them, stepping on them, and drenching them—indisputably did take place. *May 15, 2005*

===

"Let me offer a profuse apology from this network. We accidentally misspelled your name in the last hour and we are terribly sorry."

MSNBC's Gregg Jarrett apologizing on the air to black Republican consultant Niger Innis, who was identified in an on-screen graphic with a troublesome extra "g" in his first name. *February 5, 2002*

———

"Well, my analysis was wrong and I'm sorry . . . What do you want me to do? Go over and kiss the camera? What do you want me to do?"

Pugnacious pundit Bill O'Reilly begrudgingly honoring his pre–Iraq War pledge after being confronted on ABC's *Good Morning America* with videotape of him saying that if no weapons of mass destruction are found, "I will apologize to the nation and I will not trust the Bush administration again." *February 10, 2004*

———

"We want to apologize. We now have reason to believe that we made a mistake in one of our reports . . . We no longer have any evidence to support our original story. Channel 2 and I would like particularly to apologize to Marcia Clark, the District Attorney's Office, and to our viewers for this error."

KCBS-TV reporter Harvey Levin apologizing for his earlier story breathlessly suggesting that the 10:28 time stamp on a videotape of prosecutors' search of O. J. Simpson's home meant that the tape was made and filed before the search warrant had been signed at 10:45 A.M. But the time stamp just said "10:28," not "10:28 A.M." What if it had been made at 10:28 P.M.? Why, then there would be no story. *July 15, 1994*

———

"We regret the distress live images of this incident caused our viewers."
KTTV

"We did not anticipate this man's actions in time to cut away, and we deeply regret that any of our viewers saw this tragedy on our air."
KNBC, whose feed was picked up nationally by MSNBC

"KTLA shares with its viewers their distress."
KTLA news anchor Hal Fishman

"There is no mitigation—it was a mistake to show it. Period. We left our judgment at the door, and we became observers instead of journalists. We blew it."
KCOP news director Stephen Cohen

Four Los Angeles TV stations apologizing after Daniel V. Jones, who sat in his truck with his dog on a Harbor Freeway overpass for an hour in a standoff with police that was broadcast live during after-school hours, finally provided a payoff for all those years of televising live freeway chases: the truck burst into flames, Jones leaped out (leaving his dog inside), pulled off his burning clothes, got a shotgun out of the truck, and blew his head off. "We wanted to get out of it. There wasn't time," said KCOP's Cohen, though eleven seconds passed from the time Jones got his gun until he used it. "By the time we realized he was going to use the weapon on himself, we tried to get out, but we couldn't." For all the hand-wringing, no lessons were learned, and a year later a car chase that ended with a man being shot to death by police was broadcast live by KTTV, KNBC, and KTLA. *May 1, 1998*

Taking Care of Business

"We tried to humanize a cold machine and obviously it didn't work. We didn't intend to offend anyone."

Gary Mowrey, promotion director for the First Midwest Bancorp Inc., apologizing for a St. Joseph, MO, ad campaign for an ATM dubbed "Mary Anne." The slogans (among them, "What you do with Mary Anne after hours is your business" and "Mary Anne will make your nights nicer") led the local chapter of the National Organization of Women to protest the ads because they "imply that women are sex objects. They leave a very bad flavor." *April 25, 1980*

▭

"Upon reflection, I consider the comment to have been inappropriate, and apologize to anyone who may have taken offense at it."

CNN founder Ted Turner apologizing for suggesting that unemployed black Americans should be forced to work driving trailers carrying MX missiles. He explained that his comments were offered "in a lighthearted vein and certainly were not intended to insult any person or group of people." *October 30, 1981*

▭

"Obviously, it's a mistake. It's not something that we would ever have done intentionally. While we do proofread these things very carefully, with the volume on that particular page, that was something that was missed."

Jennifer Belodeau, spokeswoman for Caldor department stores, apologizing for a toys-and-games advertising supplement distributed in eighty-five Northeast newspapers that featured an image of two smiling boys sitting around a Scrabble board on which was spelled the word "RAPE." *November 3, 1998*

—

"We're really sorry for any discontent we caused."

Coca-Cola president Donald R. Keough apologizing for replacing the company's flagship soft drink with the hated "New Coke" and promising that the original flavor would soon be returning as "Coca-Cola Classic." Said Keough, "The passion for original Coke . . . was something that just flat caught us by surprise." *July 11, 1985*

—

"We are sorry that . . . any woman in the club is upset. We recognize that it was an insensitive thing."

Ron Willis, attorney for Maryland's Lakewood Country Club, apologizing for an ice sculpture in the men's locker room of a nude woman with chilled vodka spouting from between her legs. *July 18, 1996*

—

"There was a profile on me that appeared in Saturday's *Los Angeles Times*. I am enormously distressed and ashamed by

one quotation . . . For this very stupid reference I am sincerely embarrassed, and to be very honest I am just sick about it. I deeply regret this very unfortunate mistake and you have my total apology."

Southern California industrialist (and close friend of then-president Ronald Reagan) Justin Dart apologizing in a letter to Gerald Ford for telling a reporter, after spotting the former president on the plane with them, "Jerry's a nice man but he's not very smart. Actually, our seatmate is a dumb bastard." *February 7, 1982*

                        ━

"I certainly would never intend to use the offensive word in its technical sense, and I would not and could not under any circumstances question the parentage of your son, our current governor."

Justin Dart apologizing for the second time in three months for calling someone a "bastard"—this time in a letter to former governor Edmund "Pat" Brown (D-CA) for saying about his son, Gov. Edmund "Jerry" Brown (D-CA), "We've got to beat that bastard." Wrote Dart, "I have no recollection of having made this statement. However, I would not be able to flatly deny that it might have happened because I have used the word which offended Mrs. Brown and you on occasion in informal conversations when referring to other people." *May 3, 1982*

                        ━

"For my stupid and cheesy attempt at humor at the end of a luncheon interview, I apologize. It was ungracious, uncalled for . . . and inaccurate."

Vivendi-Universal co-CEO Barry Diller apologizing for referring to his longtime industry rival as "fat Marvin Davis,"
though Davis had recently lost 130 pounds. Inaccurate or not,
the insult turned up twenty months later in Davis's *Los
Angeles Times* obituary. *January 8, 2003*

**"It was not our intention to speak in a derogatory way about
the German and Japanese people."**

Jeep Bryant, spokesperson for First Union National Bank in
Charlotte, NC, apologizing for an article in the bank
newsletter that began, "The Huns and the Nips are at it again!
Fouling up our capital markets. The folks from the lands of
Teuton and Nippon jacked up their interest rates sharply in
recent months, dragging our rates along with them."
February 6, 1990

**"I did not pay enough attention to detail or to the way some
of my actions could have been perceived and my personal
style could have been perceived by certain people."**

William Aramony, president of United Way of America,
announcing his resignation as he apologized for his "lack of
sensitivity to perceptions" about the head of America's largest
charity receiving an annual income of $463,000, riding in
chauffeured limos, flying first class (at least twice on the
Concorde), and having a United Way "spin-off" corporation
buy him condominiums in New York and Florida. *February
26, 1992*

"McDonald's sincerely apologizes to Hindus, vegetarians and others for failing to provide the kind of information they needed to make informed dietary decisions at our U.S. restaurants . . . We regret we did not provide these customers with complete information and we sincerely apologize for any hardship that these miscommunications have caused among Hindus, vegetarians and others."

McDonald's apologizing for "instances in which french fries and hash browns sold at U.S. restaurants were improperly identified as 'vegetarian,'" despite the fact that they contained beef flavoring. *June 5, 2002*

—

"I've caused much harm. I've caused much grief. You are right. I did not do my job. I can only apologize for that."

Ray Brent Marsh apologizing as he received a twelve-year prison sentence for dumping 334 corpses on the property of his northwest Georgia crematorium and then passing off cement dust as their ashes. Why it was easier for him to dump the bodies and have them lying around rotting rather than cremating them—especially given that the place was, after all, a *crematorium*—went unexplained. *January 7, 2005*

—

"Our big concern is for our customers, the people who had enough faith in Chrysler to buy a vehicle from us. We did do something to have them question their faith in us. Did we screw up? You bet we did."

Chrysler CEO Lee Iacocca apologizing for his company's test driving of sixty thousand cars with the odometers disconnected, which he called "dumb," and its selling of cars damaged in test driving as new, which he said "reaches beyond dumb to stupid." *July 1, 1987*

———

"These were oratorical mistakes for which I apologize . . . I do not want these verbal mistakes to be interpreted that I am against Puerto Rico or Puerto Ricans, because I certainly am not."

J. Peter Grace, CEO of W. R. Grace & Co. and head of a presidential panel concerned with government cost cutting, apologizing for saying that "900,000 [Puerto Ricans] live in New York, and they're all on food stamps, so this food stamp program is basically a Puerto Rican program." Three days later he added that he was "deeply hurt by the misconceptions which have been created by those remarks, and specifically the accusations that I am a racist. Nothing could be further from the truth . . . I am not a racist." President Ronald Reagan's spokesman, Peter Roussel, explained that Grace was merely "expressing a personal view." *May 28, 1982*

———

"J. Peter Grace said today that language he used yesterday about Governor Cuomo and Mayor Dinkins in Milwaukee was unfortunate and he regrets having said it. Mr. Grace has apologized both to Governor Cuomo and Mayor Dinkins this morning."

Aides to J. Peter Grace announcing that their boss had apologized for saying, "Where I come from we have Cuomo the homo. And then in New York City we have Mayor Dinkins the pinkins." In letters faxed to both men Grace called his comments "unfortunate and inadvertent," adding, "It cast false aspersions on you, for which I truly apologize. It was said in jest, in the heat and excitement of the moment, and it was un-Christian and unbecoming of me." He also apologized to gays for "the inadvertent use of an offensive term . . . [While] there was no malice intended, I now realize that there is no place in our society for remarks of this kind." *October 7, 1992*

—

"Sometimes big corporations make mistakes. In this case, we did, and we've learned from it."
Taco Bell apologizing for firing Portland, OR, manager Diane King for leaving the store to help a teenager who'd been injured in a street fight. *September 11, 1995*

—

"I was a real jerk. I was greedy and stupid. I want to apologize to anyone who ever did business with me."
Travel agent Michael C. Barson apologizing in an Alexandria, VA, courtroom for defrauding thousands of people of a total of $800,000 for cheap vacations they never got to take. Barson, who actually used, among other aliases, the name "Skip Town," kept a log of bilked customers, listing next to their names the profane insults he used on them when they dared to demand their money back. *February 10, 1995*

—

"I was joking and did make a joke about the Mafia there . . . one comment lifted out of context. That one line would have

certainly been offensive to me if I were Italian. It was offensive to me as it was and I do apologize."

Ted Turner apologizing on *Larry King Live* for saying in a speech to Florida NASA employees, "Italians. Imagine the Italians at war. I mean, what a joke. They didn't belong in the last war, they were sorry they were in it, they were glad to get out of it. They'd rather be involved in crime and just making wine and having a good time." *April 21, 1986*

＝

"If it is offensive, I'm ready to say I'm just really sad and sorry. In other words, my head is bloody but unbowed . . . It slips out every now and then. I'm not trying to be offensive."

University of Kentucky trustee A. B. "Happy" Chandler apologizing for saying, during a discussion about investment in South Africa, "You know Zimbabwe's all nigger now. There aren't any whites." He explained that when he was growing up in Henderson County, "We called them 'niggers' and they didn't mind," though he added, "I know enough about what's going on in the world to know there's a lot of people who, if you call them 'nigger' now, they are going to object to it." *April 6, 1988*

＝

"I apologize to Miss Sterling and every person who has been so greatly offended."

Frank Armone, president of Marshalls department stores, apologizing for a memo posted at a cashier's counter in a Newark, CA, store instructing employees to refuse to accept returns of linen by black customers. "I have a four-year-old girl who won't stop asking, 'Why can't we do this, Mama?

Because we're black?'" said Cynthia Sterling, who was shown the memo when she attempted to return a comforter. "It's very hard to explain to her that I couldn't do something because I was black." *July 7, 1988*

⸺

"It would be irrational for anyone to think that a company that does twenty-five percent of its business in the United States would ever intentionally do anything like that."

Sony spokesperson Jason Farrow acknowledging that the Japanese company had apologized to a customer for using December 7 (Pearl Harbor Day) as the example in a manual showing how to set the date on its VCRs. *April 2, 1990*

⸺

"The excerpt . . . is offensive and, therefore, had no place in any General Motors activities."

General Motors chairman Robert Stempel apologizing for referring to a Japanese-made vehicle in a promotional video as a "little faggot truck." *November 9, 1990*

⸺

"I want everyone to know that the company views these events as deplorable. American Airlines apologizes to anyone who was offended by the unfortunate actions of the few employees involved in this unhappy incident. Their actions do not reflect American Airlines' policy or practice, and everyone has my pledge that we will do everything possible to ensure that such lapses in judgment do not occur in the future."

American Airlines CEO Robert Crandall apologizing for the

flight crew that changed all the pillows and blankets on a flight continuing on to California after several attendees of a gay-rights rally in Washington, D.C., disembarked in Dallas. *April 29, 1993*

—

"We sincerely apologize for this error. We did not intend to offend anyone. Please forgive us for this mistake."

Chicago's Glenview State Bank apologizing for a customer newsletter, written by the bank's president, that praised Adolf Hitler for his economic policies in the 1930s. *July 29, 2003*

—

"Let me say once again, for everyone to hear, I despise Hitler and everything he stood for. I can't tell you how much I regret my insensitivity on this point. It was innocent, but it was very, very bad judgment and it was in very bad taste. I now realize that and I deeply regret it and apologize for it."

Ralph Engelstad, owner of the Imperial Palace Hotel and Casino in Las Vegas, apologizing for conducting two parties celebrating Adolf Hitler's birthday and for maintaining a Nazi memorabilia room at the resort. *October 6, 1988*

—

"It was never our intention to offend anyone with this exhibition and we sincerely regret any offense that was taken."

Manhattan clothing store Barneys apologizing for artist Tom Sachs's "Hello Kitty Nativity Scene" window display, in which the three wise men were depicted as three Bart Simpsons, the baby Jesus was a Hello Kitty doll with a halo, and the Virgin Mary was a pregnant Hello Kitty doll decked out like Madonna (the singer, not the religious icon) in a leather bondage outfit (nipples showing) with her legs spread apart. *December 13, 1994*

———

"I really, from the very bottom of my heart, want to apologize for statements I made about Christianity. I did it mainly out of frustration. At one time or another, I've offended almost every group. I'm sure I'll be apologizing again."

Ted Turner apologizing for repeatedly calling Christianity "a religion for losers." *June 13, 1990*

———

"I admit there can be no valid excuse for what I did. I grew up side by side with black people. Many are my dear friends. My apology is to them and all others who I have wrongfully offended."

Newport News, VA, Nissan dealer Bob Crumpler, who was caught (on a videotape made by a former employee who quit because he couldn't take Crumpler's verbal abuse) referring to a black worker as a "nigger," apologizing on his own videotape. Crumpler, who had recently settled a lawsuit brought by a black woman who said he closed a car door on her arm and called her a "nigger," promised viewers of his apology video, "My future actions will reflect a better approach for Bob Crumpler in his personnel and business actions." *December 13, 1996*

———

"I want to offer an apology to our fellow employees who were rightly offended by these statements . . . and to people throughout America and elsewhere around the world."

Texaco chairman Peter Bijur apologizing after audiotapes surfaced in which company executives made fun of Hanukkah and Kwanzaa and referred to black employees as "niggers" and "black jelly beans." *November 6, 1996*

⸺

"I do have regrets. I have sincere regrets that many of the things we are now embarked on doing could have been done sooner. To the extent any of those things either changed your decision not to quit or would have allowed you to quit smoking sooner, or not to have taken up smoking in the first place, then I sincerely apologize to you."

Brown & Williamson CEO Nicholas Brookes apologizing in a Miami courtroom to people ravaged by tobacco-related ailments who joined a class action lawsuit against the industry for having consistently and relentlessly denied that smoking is harmful and addictive. *June 15, 2000*

⸺

"For one of our tobacco companies to commission this study was not just a terrible mistake, it was wrong . . . [It] exhibited terrible judgment as well as a complete and unacceptable disregard of basic human values . . . All of us at Philip Morris, no matter where we work, are extremely sorry for this. No one benefits from the very real, serious and significant diseases caused by smoking."

Philip Morris apologizing for a report prepared by Arthur D. Little International on the economy of the Czech Republic that found "indirect positive effects" of cigarette smoking—the huge sums of money (for health care, pensions, and housing) the government saves thanks to the early deaths of smokers. *July 26, 2001*

⸺

"I come before you to apologize to you, the American people, and especially to the families who have lost loved ones in these terrible rollover accidents. I also come to accept full and personal responsibility on behalf of Bridgestone Firestone for the events that led to this hearing."

CEO Masatoshi Ono apologizing for dozens of accidents (resulting in scores of deaths and hundreds of injuries) widely believed to have been caused by his company's faulty tires. A month later he explained that this was merely "a sympathy expressed for those individuals who operated vehicles using our products and got into accidents" and by no means an admission that those accidents were caused by his defective tires: "If we are deemed responsible for the accidents, that is another matter. However, there are maybe outside causes that had caused the accidents. Then, I wouldn't say we're responsible for those accidents." *September 6, 2000*

⸺

"I made some statements that were inappropriate during an open and frank discussion with *Vanity Fair*. In particular the term 'gay mafia' does not reflect my true feelings or attitudes. It is regrettable and I am truly sorry."

Former talent agent Michael Ovitz apologizing for blaming his spectacular, decade-long career flameout not on his own preternatural penchant for self-destruction but, rather, on the coordinated efforts of his Hollywood enemies, many but by no means all of whom were homosexual. *July 2, 2002*

━━

"I certainly understand our employees' concern about their privacy and I want to assure them that only the top half of one locker was intended to be shown and not the entire locker room . . . I apologize for the disturbance to our employees and medical staff."

Sister Jean Louise, president of Maryland's Holy Cross Hospital, apologizing for an incorrectly installed surveillance camera meant to monitor a nurse suspected of drug abuse that instead broadcast a full view of the women's locker room over the in-hospital television system. *March 26, 1987*

━━

"Somehow they fell through the system. I apologize, I sincerely apologize."

Scuba instructor Karl Jesienowski apologizing for his tour boat's having returned to shore from a diving cruise at Australia's Great Barrier Reef without an American couple whose absence was only noticed two days later when crew members found their belongings still on the boat. *January 30, 1998*

━━

"I really am sorry. It's the biggest pain in my life . . . I'm sorry they had problems. I'm dreadfully sorry and everybody in my family is."

Charles H. Keating Jr., chairman of the failed Lincoln Savings and Loan of Los Angeles, apologizing for his involvement in America's worst-ever savings and loan collapse. *May 9, 1990*

⸗

"We really apologize to our customers that merchandise in some of our stores has been signed incorrectly as 'Made in U.S.A.' even though labels on each garment were clearly marked as imported items."

Wal-Mart president and CEO David Glass rushing to get his apology on the record mere hours before a *Dateline NBC* exposé of the company's more questionable practices. *December 22, 1992*

⸗

"I hope you and all those offended by this comment will accept my deepest apology . . . The comparison I made referred only to the way Hitler managed the news in Germany. I regret this comment and assure you it was not intended to offend nor to trivialize the role of an individual who wreaked so much havoc upon the Jewish people."

Ted Turner (who a year earlier had said that not owning a major television network made him "feel like, oh, those Jewish people in Germany in 1942") apologizing in a letter to the Anti-Defamation League for comparing News Corp. chairman Rupert Murdoch to the "late Fuhrer." *October 1, 1996*

⸗

"I apologize for any misunderstanding, and if we have offended anyone in the disabled community."

Bill Ross, Disneyland's VP of public affairs, apologizing after it was reported that the park had ended its twenty-year-old Happy Hearts program catering to children with special needs. Reaction was so hostile that Disney officials not only couldn't eliminate the program—in which the handicapped and their families got a 50 percent admission discount—but also were forced by the demands of PR to double the annual number of days of eligibility from twelve to twenty-four. *March 24, 1997*

"We're very sorry that this situation occurred . . . A mistake was made, and we're doing what we can to make things right."

Chevron USA executive Bill Walters apologizing to two troops of handicapped Boy Scouts for his company's having pressured them to dismantle their Christmas tree lot—where they were selling trees to make money for summer camp— because their sales tent blocked a Chevron sign at the next-door gas station. *December 7, 1987*

"The editors of *Focus* magazine apologize to our readers and, in particular, to people of color for an illustration that perpetuates racial stereotypes."

AT&T apologizing via e-mail to recipients of the corporation's in-house magazine, which featured a cartoon showing the world with callers on various continents talking on their phones, all human except for the African caller, depicted as an ape. *September 16, 1993*

"We did determine that some of these historical images may be offensive to our North American readers . . . We never seek to hurt employees. We did apologize for any pain or embarrassment we might have caused anyone."

Jim Morton, spokesman for the North American subsidiary of France's Michelin tire company, apologizing for the inclusion in a book commemorating the hundredth anniversary of the Michelin Man logo of a drawing of a big-breasted black woman nursing the baby Michelin Man and one of a mule with the face of a black man. *March 17, 1998*

—

"We apologize to the students and chaperones who did not feel welcome during their visit . . . It is clear that these customers do not believe they were treated with the courtesy and respect that we pledge to every Denny's guest. For that, we are sorry."

John A. Romandetti, president of the Denny's restaurant chain—which four years earlier shelled out $46 million to settle a discrimination lawsuit filed by black Secret Service agents who said they were denied service at a Denny's in Annapolis, MD—apologizing to black sixth graders who said they were denied service at a Denny's in Ocoee, FL. *May 5, 1998*

—

"The mere existence of the document is inexcusable . . . As a Latino, I myself am offended. But as a thirty-year veteran of American Airlines, I can attest to the fact that this document is not reflective of the attitudes that exist within our company."

American Airlines senior VP Peter Dolara apologizing for a section in the company's pilot training guide called "Survival in Latin America," which said of passengers in the region, "They expect not to depart on time. In fact, it's rumored that they will call in a false bomb threat to delay a departure if they think they'll be late," and "They like a drink in the plane prior to takeoff. Unruly and-or intoxicated passengers are not infrequent." *August 20, 1997*

———

"Mr. Ted Turner deeply regrets offending the Polish people during a speech he made in Washington, D.C. last week. He has great respect for Poland and its people and extends his heartfelt apologies to them."

Turner Broadcasting System apologizing for its chief's response when asked what he would say to Pope John Paul II if they were to meet. Turned out he would ask, "Ever seen a Polish mine detector?" and point to his foot. *February 21, 1999*

———

"I would like to say we're really sorry. You did meet up with one very, very rigid staff person."

Robert Chavez, CEO of Hermès USA, apologizing to Oprah Winfrey for an incident at the Paris store in which she showed up at closing time and an employee refused to let her in to shop. *September 19, 2005*

———

"We have a long and diverse record of supporting disabled athletes, and we're extremely and sincerely apologetic."

Nike spokesman Lee Weinstein apologizing for a magazine ad for the ACG Air Dri-Goat that read, "Right about now you're probably asking yourself, 'How can a trail running shoe with an outer sole designed like a goat's hoof help me avoid compressing my spinal cord into a Slinky on the side of some unsuspecting conifer, thereby rendering me a drooling, misshapen non-extreme-trail-running husk of my former self, forced to roam the earth in a motorized wheelchair with my name, embossed on one of those cute little license plates you get at carnivals or state fairs, fastened to the back?'" The ad was created by the Portland, OR, agency Wieden & Kennedy, producers of the quickly yanked Olympics TV spot that featured runner Suzy Favor Hamilton being chased by a chainsaw-wielding maniac. *October 25, 2000*

—

"The tone of one portion of the memo was regrettable, and TCI has extended its apologies to the FCC. TCI has not engaged in a pattern of blaming either the FCC or the Congress for increases, if any, in prices for unregulated services or transactions."

Tele-Communications Inc., America's largest cable operator, apologizing to regulators for a memo by TCI employee Barry Marshall encouraging managers to raise rates for things like service calls and installations. "The best news of all," he wrote, "is we can blame it on re-regulation and the government now. Let's take advantage of it!" *November 16, 1993*

—

"Microsoft Mexico offers an apology to its users and to the public in general for some grave errors in the synonyms of the Microsoft Word dictionary in Spanish, whose mistaken connotations are offensive."

Microsoft apologizing for several unfortunate entries in its Spanish-language thesaurus for Word 6.0. Among them: synonyms for "Indian" included "savage" and "man-eater," synonyms for "lesbian" included "vicious" and "pervert," and synonyms for "black" included "cannibal" and "barbarian." Synonyms for "Western" included "white" and "civilized." *July 5, 1996*

—

"I take full responsibility for my actions. I also accept that there are various personal issues that I need to address and have started taking the difficult, yet necessary, steps to resolve them. I want to apologize to all of the people I have let down because of my behavior which has reflected badly on my family, friends, co-workers, business associates and others."

Model Kate Moss apologizing after her videotaped coke snorting led H&M, Chanel, and Burberry to cancel their contracts with her. *September 22, 2005*

—

"To say that I chose the wrong words in describing Detroit workers in my interview with *Fortune* magazine is an understatement. And I apologize for that, especially to those who work for Chrysler."

Chrysler CEO Lee Iacocca apologizing for lamenting the difficulty of finding drug-free autoworkers in Detroit. *March 22, 1991*

—

"I want to apologize to the people of the Pittsburgh area for the inconvenience they have suffered as the result of this incident."

John Hall, chairman of Ashland Oil, apologizing for the collapse of a diesel fuel tank that sent a million-gallon oil slick flowing down Pennsylvania's Monongahela River. *January 5, 1988*

—

"I am very sorry for this happening. I don't know what else to say. I think it was a very bad time and all else is in your hands."

Georgios Vlahos, chief mate of the Greek tanker *World Prodigy*, apologizing to a federal board of inquiry for his ship's running aground and spilling 420,000 gallons of heating oil off the coast of Rhode Island. *June 30, 1989*

—

"Southern Pacific and the 10,000 California employees that we have in our company are deeply sorry this happened. We could not believe that this combination of events, defying the odds, could end up with this kind of problem."

Southern Pacific Railroad apologizing for a seven-car derailment in which the car containing 19,000 gallons of the extremely toxic metam-sodium pesticide was the only one to land in the Sacramento River. *July 20, 1991*

—

"It's a very serious condition. It's one we regret. It's one that should not have happened."

Unocal executive vice president John F. Imle Jr. apologizing for leaking 8.5 million gallons of petroleum thinner into the ocean just south of San Luis Obispo over a forty-year period—the largest oil spill in California history. *March 15, 1994*

       =

"I do apologize for what's happened. I don't know what apology would be appropriate, though. I could apologize to the people of Alaska, and I mean that from the bottom of my heart, but I still don't think it would be enough."

Captain Joseph Hazelwood apologizing on the occasion of the tenth anniversary of the 10-million-gallon *Exxon Valdez* oil spill, the worst in U.S. history. Though much was made of how many drinks he'd had that night, he was not the man at the wheel when the ship ran aground. That was Robert Kagan, whose steering abilities Hazelwood had been wary of (though obviously not wary enough). While Kagan believed that Hazelwood commended him after the accident, a witness at his 1990 trial testified that the captain's comment—"Damn fine job, Bob"—was actually "kind of dark humor." *March 24, 1999*

       =

"It's totally inconsistent with the kind of behavior we would have expected from our people, so it has been very upsetting to learn of this."

Starbucks president Orin Smith talking to the Associated Press after apologizing to rescue workers who ran into a lower Manhattan Starbucks on September 11 to get water to treat shock victims, only to be charged $130 by employees for three cases of bottled water. *September 25, 2001*

       =

"I apologize to all Christians for my comment about Catholics wearing ashes on their foreheads on Ash Wednesday. I do not believe in any form of prejudice or discrimination, especially religious intolerance . . . Please accept my apology for any pain my thoughtless comment may have caused Catholics and all Christians."

CNN founder Ted Turner apologizing for referring to those network employees who showed up to work with smudged foreheads as "Jesus freaks." *March 9, 2001*

═══

"I apologize to whoever I need to apologize to. This was a mistake, a very unfortunate mistake."

Herbert Miller, VP for sales at Texas-based Merit Industries, apologizing for an error made by his company while fulfilling an order for a commemorative plaque commissioned by a Florida company to be presented to actor James Earl Jones at a Martin Luther King Jr. birthday celebration. Unfortunately, the plaque as manufactured read, "Thank you James Earl Ray for keeping the dream alive." *January 16, 2002*

I Fought the Law

"I'd like to apologize to the San Francisco Police Department for offending them in any way. All I can say is, I left my heart in San Francisco."

Porn star Marilyn Chambers apologizing after being arrested for letting audience members at her live show, "Feel the Magic," touch her naked body with their hands and mouths. *February 4, 1985*

—

"My intention was never to hurt the public. I would like to apologize."

Antoine Yates apologizing to a Manhattan judge for keeping a four-hundred-pound tiger and a five-foot-long alligator in his fifth-floor Harlem apartment. Yates, whose mauling by the tiger attracted police attention, explained that he was "trying to create a Garden of Eden, something that this world lacks." Said his sister, "He just has a love for animals. There's nothing wrong with that." *October 7, 2004*

—

"I just want to say how absolutely sorry I am that innocent people got hurt that night. Please tell them and please tell

their families how terrible I feel. I've felt this way since this happened."

Manhattan publicist Lizzie Grubman talking to the press outside Suffolk County Court after her hearing on charges of assault, vehicular assault, driving under the influence, and leaving the scene of an accident. (Reacting badly to being told she couldn't park her Mercedes SUV in the fire lane of a Southampton nightspot, she had furiously gunned the car in reverse into a crowd of clubgoers before driving off.) *July 19, 2002*

"I am sorry for what I have done. I love music and don't want to hurt the artists I love."

Preteen Brianna LaHara, one of 261 people sued by the Recording Industry Association of America for pirating music over the Internet, apologizing for downloading such songs as "If You're Happy and You Know It" and the theme to the sitcom *Family Matters*. She was allowed to settle for two thousand dollars and the above apology. *September 9, 2003*

"Dear people of Oklahoma, I offer my apology and ask that you forgive me. I shamefully admit I've broken many laws. My actions and inactions have hurt many people . . . I deeply regret not taking the information I had to the police. Dear people, please, I offer my apology and I ask you to forgive me . . . Please, please don't let thoughts of me continue to hurt you."

Michael J. Fortier at his sentencing hearing in Oklahoma City, after listening to three hours of testimony by people about how their lives and thousands of others were ruined by the 168-deaths-and-500-plus-injuries disaster that he could have prevented if he'd only made one phone call to warn the authorities that his friends Timothy McVeigh and Terry Nichols were planning to blow up the Alfred P. Murrah Federal Building. "I should have let the police judge his intentions," Fortier said of McVeigh. "Clearly I could not. I sometimes daydream that I did do this, and I became a hero, but reality is that I am not." Said one surviving relative about Fortier's twelve-year sentence (of which three had already been served), "I think it should have been more." *May 28, 1998*

⸗

"I wish I knew words to tell you how sorry I am and how much regret and pain I feel. I'm so sorry. I'm a different person now. I made terrible choices."

Hollywood madam Heidi Fleiss apologizing to the federal judge who sentenced her to thirty-seven months in prison for money laundering and tax evasion. *January 7, 1997*

⸗

"I did break our nation's laws. I allowed myself to get too caught up in what I was doing to consider the consequences or to stop myself from doing what I knew was wrong. For that I am truly sorry and ashamed."

Former Drexel Burnham Lambert junk-bond dealer Michael Milken apologizing in a letter to U.S. District Judge Kimba Wood after pleading guilty to six felony counts of violating federal conspiracy, tax, and securities laws. *November 5, 1990*

⸗

"I want to publicly admit that I caused a mouse to be placed in a can of Coors beer and acknowledge the wrongdoing of that act . . . I have no one to blame but myself."

Unemployed construction worker James Harvey apologizing in a Jacksonville, FL, court, where he received an eighteen-month prison sentence for product tampering and extortion. *October 25, 1988*

—

"I wanted to win, and the numbers were so overwhelming. I wanted to win so bad for my kids and my family, and I apologize to anyone who was inconvenienced. I wanted it so bad to change my life. It just took over me."

Elecia Battle of Cleveland apologizing for falsely claiming that she'd bought and lost a winning Mega Millions lottery ticket worth $162 million. *January 8, 2004*

—

"I stand here today still in disbelief of my wrongdoing. Money or greed was never the motive. I suffered from an illness and I was sick."

Former pharmaceutical executive Francis X. Vitale Jr. apologizing for embezzling $12.5 million from the New Jersey–based Engelhard Corp. and spending it on antique clocks. *January 15, 1998*

—

"My sympathy goes out to the Byrd family. There is no reason for a person to take the life of another, and to take it in such a manner is beyond any kind of reasoning. It hurts me deeply to know that a boy I raised and considered to be

the most loved boy I knew could find it in himself to take a life. This deed cannot be undone, but I hope we can all find it in our hearts to go forward in peace, and with love for all. Let us find in our hearts love for our fellow man. Hate can only destroy. Again I want to say I'm sorry."

Ronald King, father of John William King, apologizing for his son's involvement in the murder-by-dragging-behind-a-truck of James Byrd Jr. in Jasper, TX. *June 10, 1998*

"I apologize for my behavior. I am shamed by it. Beyond its illegality, I have torn the trust of so many. Worse, I have opened the door for calumny against my totally innocent wife and our children. I have hurt them deeply. I have hurt so many deeply."

Former FBI agent Robert Hanssen apologizing in an Alexandria, VA, courtroom as he was sentenced to life in prison for spying for the Russians. *May 10, 2002*

"I deeply regret the anguish which I have caused."

Former *Wall Street Journal* reporter R. Foster Winans apologizing in a letter to his editors for abusing his position as co-writer of the influential Heard on the Street column by tipping his stockbroker in advance about the contents of upcoming columns. *March 26, 1985*

"I can't say anything except that I am totally sorry and feel nothing but remorse for having caused that tragic death."

Sirhan Sirhan apologizing in an interview with David Frost

for killing Robert F. Kennedy, explaining that he bore him no personal malice but did it only to protect the Palestinians. *February 14, 1989*

—

"I did take some lives and I'm very sorry for that."

David "Son of Sam" Berkowitz apologizing in a prison TV interview with *Inside Edition* for his 1977 murder spree, explaining that the point of the shootings "was to bring chaos to the city . . . bringing the city of New York to its knees and so forth." *November 7, 1993*

—

"She apologizes to her husband, Barry Aron, for her conduct, the cause of which she is just starting to understand."

Barry Helfand, defense lawyer for Montgomery County, MD, Planning Board member Ruthann Aron, relating his client's regret and bewilderment at having tried to hire a hit man to kill her husband. *September 9, 1997*

—

"I apologize. I do understand that everyone should have to pay the tolls."

Orlando scofflaw Wesley Ridgwell apologizing for a ten-month spree of barreling through more than seven hundred Florida tollbooths without paying. His Honda (with its JST CRZY vanity plate) was photographed each time and, though he had initially claimed that someone had stolen his license plate and put it on a similar-looking vehicle, he agreed to pay more than seven thousand dollars in fines. *November 28, 2000*

⸺

"I'm so sorry for what I did to you and your family, especially to Gary and his name and how I took six years away from him, and I really want your forgiveness, especially Gary's forgiveness."

Cathleen Crowell Webb apologizing to Chicagoan Barbara Dotson (who forgave her) via split screen on NBC's *Today Show* for falsely accusing her son of rape in 1977 because— then sixteen—she was afraid her boyfriend had gotten her pregnant. Gary Dotson was convicted and had served six years of a twenty-five-to-fifty-year sentence before Webb's conscience made her come forward. (Gary also forgave her, though several weeks later, in a joint appearance with her on the *CBS Morning News*, he declined host Phyllis George's invitation to give Webb a hug.) *March 29, 1985*

⸺

"I apologize to the court and the American people for my involvement in this group, and I regret it very much."

Former white supremacist turned government witness Denver Parmenter Jr. apologizing in a Portland, OR, courtroom for his longtime ties to the Order, an ultraviolent neo-Nazi group. Parmenter, who received a twenty-year sentence for his role in the group's efforts to overthrow the federal government, said he decided to cooperate with the FBI after he realized through Bible study that he'd been acting against God. *February 19, 1986*

⸺

"I wish to inform the court that I remain truly sorry for the tragedy that happened in 1971. I feel that due to my mental state at the time, I was unaccountable for what happened.

**I ask all those who were affected by this for their forgive-
ness, their understanding, and their prayers."**

John Emil List apologizing in a New Jersey court before being
sentenced to five consecutive life sentences for shooting his
entire family to death in their home. In a letter left at the
crime scene, List—a devout Lutheran—had explained that he
killed his wife because she'd stopped going to church, that he
killed his three teenagers before they could stop going to
church, and that he killed his mother because she wouldn't
have wanted to live once everyone else was dead. List, whose
arrest almost eighteen years after the murders came as a
result of a tip called in to the Fox program *America's Most
Wanted*, had recently remarried. *May 1, 1990*

**"Each day I am understanding more about who I am and
the issues that influenced me to respond inappropriately.
Therefore, I have started professional treatment, voluntarily.
I am truly sorry for the troubles I caused, and I offer my
deep and sincere apology."**

Runaway bride Jennifer Wilbanks apologizing in a statement
read by her pastor for having taken a cross-country Grey-
hound bus trip days before her scheduled Georgia wedding
and then called home claiming to have been kidnapped by a
Hispanic man and a white woman in a van. *May 5, 2005*

**"Your Honor, for the last two and a half years, I have been
knowing this day would come. How things happen, why
things happen, we don't always know. But I would like to
apologize for what did happen. There were a lot of human**

factors. There were a lot of victims. The banks, for example.
I apologize to them. And certainly to the bank officers.
Banks are people too. I let them down, for which I'm eternally sorry . . . I can't believe I have to apologize to my own
children. I apologize to my attorneys, who haven't been paid
for a long time, for basically two years. They have stood by
me through all of this. Oddly enough, I would like to apologize to the people of the city of Los Angeles. When you own
a professional sports team, as I did, you do have a certain
duty to the public. We tried to do something special with this
franchise. I apologize for the way we went about it. Finally,
Your Honor, I've lost pretty much everything, materially, in
my life. Everything I had as a child, everything I ever wanted
or got, in the end, it didn't turn out to be worth much. In a
funny way, I've learned a lot. I've learned that those things
are not very important, the baubles and such. I've learned
what really counts, like whatever time I could spend now
with my children. With that, thank you."

> Former Los Angeles Kings owner Bruce McNall apologizing
> to the judge who went on to sentence him to almost six years
> in prison for his $236 million worth of financial shenani-
> gans, the victims of which included six banks, a securities
> firm, and his own hockey team. *January 9, 1997*

"Peace and love. I'm sorry for the damage that occurred to
the Liberty Bell."

> Longtime drifter Mitchell Guilliatt apologizing for the chip-
> ping and denting of a national icon that occurred when he
> found himself in Philadelphia with a small sledgehammer.
> *June 21, 2001*

━━

"I am very sorry to the country and sorry for the crime I committed against America. I do want to say I am not a spy. My actions . . . were out of desperation and stupidity."

Randy Miles Jeffries, a messenger for a Washington, D.C., company that transcribed sensitive congressional hearings, apologizing for trying to sell classified documents to the Soviets in order to solve his desperate problem of not having enough money to take his wife on a vacation. "That's why he did it," said his lawyer, G. Allen Dale, "not to sell out his country." *March 13, 1986*

━━

"I have had a long period of time in isolation to reflect on my conduct. I am guilty and I accept full responsibility. To the victims, I am extremely sorry."

Kansas City, MO, pharmacist Robert R. Courtney apologizing for diluting—on 158 occasions—the cancer drugs taken by thirty-four patients. *February 26, 2002*

━━

"I sincerely apologize for what happened . . . I promise to do well at the Center for Drug-Free Living from now on."

Florida governor Jeb Bush's handcuffed twenty-five-year-old daughter Noelle apologizing just before receiving a ten-day jail sentence for being found with a chunk of crack in her shoe during her court-ordered stint at a rehab. This followed by three months another rehab incident in which she got three days in jail for possessing an unauthorized prescription drug. *October 18, 2002*

—

"I feel an apology is in order to this court. I would like to extend that to you. When I was here in this court, I was ventilating a great deal of anger."

Hustler publisher Larry Flynt apologizing to black U.S. District Court Judge Consuelo Marshall for calling her a "nigger" during a hearing on charges that he desecrated the American flag when he wore it to court as a diaper. *September 6, 1984*

—

"Your Honor, I can only express the deepest feeling of remorse, shame, sorrow, and humiliation, after having had the privilege of serving in so many distinguished positions, to come to this in the twilight of my life."

Former U.S. Treasury secretary Robert Anderson apologizing at his sentencing for income tax evasion and illegal operation of an unregistered offshore bank. *June 25, 1987*

—

"I dishonored myself. I devastated my family. Nobody could be any sorrier."

Retired Navy officer Arthur J. Walker, sentenced to life in prison, apologizing for the seven counts of espionage he was found guilty of. *November 12, 1985*

—

"What I did as an act of revenge was wrong in every way. I only ask that you forgive me for resorting to such despicable behavior, which is disgraceful. I was wrong and I committed a terrible sin. How did I let hatred invade my heart and guide my actions?"

New Jersey developer Charles Kushner apologizing in a letter to his sister, Esther Schulder, for getting back at her husband—who was cooperating with a federal investigation of Kushner's finances—by hiring a prostitute for him and then sending Esther a videotape of the encounter. *August 31, 2004*

—

"I'm really sorry for what happened. I'd like to say I'm sorry to the McBurnett family. If there's anything I could ever say or do to bring back Leo, I would."

Telephone repairman Andrew Burnett apologizing in a San Jose, CA, courtroom for reacting to a minor fender bender with Nevada real estate agent Sara McBurnett—he cut her off on a rainy night in heavy airport traffic, causing her Subaru Legacy to graze the bumper of his GMC SUV—by charging out of his vehicle, reaching into hers when she rolled down her window to apologize, grabbing her bichon frise from her lap, and hurling him into traffic, where he was run over before his owner's horrified eyes. The judge, finding his apology insincere, sentenced him to three years in state prison, where fellow inmates nicknamed him "Poodle Boy." *July 13, 2001*

—

"I would like to say to all of you, the Thornton family and Jerry Dean's family, that I am so sorry. I hope God will give you peace with this. I love all of you very much. I am going to be face to face with Jesus now. I will see you all when you get there. I will wait for you."

Born-again drug-crazed killer Karla Faye Tucker apologizing

to the families of the two victims she hacked to death in 1983 from the gurney where she lay with needles poised to pump poison into each of her arms after Texas governor George W. Bush ignored her pleas for mercy (and later mimicked those pleas while being interviewed by a writer for the magazine *Talk*). Her nationally celebrated death row religious conversion was convincing enough to inspire televangelist Pat Robertson, Pope John Paul II, and Ron Carlson (the brother of one of the victims) to ask that her life be spared. As Carlson put it afterward, "She was a perfect example of how rehabilitation in the penal system is supposed to work. And what did they do? They executed her." *February 3, 1998*

You Can't Say That on the Radio

"Every entertainer and satirist has at one time or another said something that he or she wishes he could take back. My attempted humor on Martin Luther King Day was reprehensible, and I'm glad I have the chance to look you in the eye and say that I'm sorry."

Washington, D.C., shock jock Doug ("the Greaseman") Tracht apologizing in a videotaped statement for joking, on the first celebration of the federal holiday honoring the birth of Martin Luther King Jr., that if assassinating a black leader resulted in a day off, "Kill four more and we can take a whole week off." *February 7, 1986*

—

"WNEW regrets the unfortunate incident that took place. We apologize to anyone who has been offended, and have taken measures to ensure that it does not happen again."

Ken Stevens, general manager of New York's formerly great WNEW-FM, apologizing for a segment in which shock jocks Opie and Anthony (fired by Infinity Broadcasting because of this stunt) aired an eyewitness description of a Virginia couple having sex in a vestibule in St. Patrick's Cathedral while worshippers prayed nearby. *August 16, 2002*

—

"We would like to say publicly what employees involved were told then: This incident was inappropriate and unacceptable. The promotion could be viewed as offensive and derogatory. We sincerely apologize to our employees and anyone else for any offense that has been taken."

Steven Bornstein, president of Disney's ABC broadcast division, apologizing—in the face of threatened license challenges and national boycotts—for a year-old promotion on Los Angeles radio station KLOS involving on-the-air giveaways of plastic gardening tools called "Black Hoes." Three black women who worked at the station filed lawsuits against Disney, claiming that the promotion had the "conscious aim and intent of providing racially offensive, sexually charged entertainment for its primarily white male listening audience and advertising clients." With the likes of Johnnie Cochran and Jesse Jackson getting involved, Disney paid $3.5 million to make the lawsuits go away. *August 24, 1999*

—

"We apologize. We didn't think it was going to go this far."

Los Angeles morning DJ Kevin Ryder apologizing on behalf of himself and his partner, Gene "Bean" Baxter, for fabricating and airing a phony confession by a man who claimed to have beaten his girlfriend to death. The Los Angeles County Sheriff's Department billed KROQ for the more than twelve thousand dollars spent during a ten-month investigation of the uncommitted crime. *April 12, 1991*

—

"Our thoughtless act has caused a great deal of pain and anger for us all."

Don Howe, general manager of KBPI in Denver, apologizing in an ad in the *Denver Post* for the actions of morning-show DJs Roger Beaty and Dean Myers, whose response to Nuggets guard Mahmoud Abdul-Rauf's refusal to stand for "The Star-Spangled Banner" before a basketball game was to send three people with horns into a local Muslim mosque and broadcast the incident live as they harassed worshippers by blaring a trumpet-and-bugle version of the anthem. *March 30, 1996*

"It's probably not something to kid around about. I apologize to the Iranian people who were offended."

Shock jock Don Imus apologizing for saying, "Who cares?" when told of the crash of an Iranian airliner that killed forty-three. *February 14, 2004*

"As you all know, I'm a satirical person. My comments about Selena's tragic death, without a doubt, were not made with the intention of causing even more pain to her family, friends, and those who loved her."

Howard "King of All Media" Stern apologizing (originally in Spanish) for making fun of the murder of the Mexican pop star by playing her music with the accompanying sounds of gunfire. Further disparaging the Selena oeuvre, Stern had said, "Alvin and the Chipmunks have more soul," adding, "Spanish people have the worst taste in music." *April 6, 1995*

⸻

"I apologize a thousand times."

Air America radio host Randi Rhodes apologizing for "bad taste" after following a mention of George W. Bush's Social Security policies by saying, "Well, here's your answer, you ungrateful whelp," and playing the sound of a shotgun firing three times. *April 27, 2005*

⸻

"It's an instance we would like to put behind us."

Beverly Rice, general manager of WDEZ in Wausau, WI, apologizing for country music DJ Terry T, who had asked listeners to call in with jokes about the Auschwitz death camp on the fiftieth anniversary of its liberation. *January 31, 1995*

⸻

"I apologize if what I did was fearful to some people who don't advocate nuking everybody over there."

St. Louis, MO, DJ John Ulett apologizing for broadcasting a mock news bulletin that America was under nuclear attack, the intent of which was "to jolt people"—particularly the people who'd been calling in to his show advocating nuking Iraq—into contemplating the true horror of nuclear war. *January 29, 1991*

⸻

"I didn't intend to do this harm to anyone. I'm sorry. The station is sorry."

University of California, Santa Cruz, student Roger Takacs apologizing for creating panic on his campus by broadcasting a program on the college radio station falsely claiming that a

major earthquake had just killed thousands in Los Angeles.
February 26, 1993

=

"Last night, this radio station erroneously reported an incident involving Britney Spears and Justin Timberlake. The Eagle apologizes for any confusion this erroneous report may have caused."

Dallas rock station KEGL apologizing for its DJs Kramer and Twitch having "erroneously reported" that teen stars Britney Spears and Justin Timberlake had been killed in a Los Angeles car crash. (Before landing at "the Eagle," Kramer and Twitch worked at KSJO in San Jose, CA, where they were suspended for encouraging those listening in cars to run over bicyclists and motorcyclists, or at least to mess with them by swinging open their car doors.) *June 13, 2001*

=

"As CEO of Clear Channel Radio, I do not support or condone the anti-cyclists' messages and have taken steps to ensure they do not occur again."

Clear Channel president John Hogan apologizing for shock jocks on three Clear Channel stations who urged listeners in cars to run down people on bikes. *November 5, 2003*

=

"Unfortunately, I used inappropriate words in describing my concerns. These concerns, especially when taken out of context, sound insensitive and unfeeling. That was never my intent."

Dallas radio talk host David Gold apologizing to his listeners for saying that eighteen illegal aliens who suffocated in a boxcar "got what they deserved." Asked Adelfa Callejo, chairwoman of the Coalition of Hispanic Organizations, "How can 'They deserve to die' be taken out of context?" *July 21, 1987*

"Unfortunately, we did not realize the impact our statements would have on Don's friends and family members."

Evansville, IN, morning DJ Brad Booker apologizing on the WSTO Web site for an April Fool's Day prank in which he and cohost Diane Douglas said that their thoughts and prayers were with the locally based family of New York Yankees batting coach Don Mattingly, thus terrifying his two young sons, who assumed something had happened to their father on his way back from the team's trip to Japan. Booker explained they had planned to reveal "later in the morning" that they "were concerned" for Mattingly because they'd heard "he had nicked himself shaving." Station general manager Tim Huelsing said the DJs "understand the severity of this mistake" and "they have assured me that it won't happen again. It won't happen again." *April 2, 2004*

"Regrettably, some of the words I've used have hurt some people, and I am sorry for that. Words that I have used in a clinical context have been perceived as judgment. They were not meant to characterize homosexual individuals or encourage others to disparage homosexuals. I regularly remind my listeners that we are all made in God's image and, therefore, we should treat one another with love and kindness, irrespective of one's faith."

Dr. Laura Schlessinger regretting referring to homosexuality as a "biological error" and "deviant" (as in, "Gay rights? Why does deviant sexual behavior get rights?") on her radio talk show—a pseudo-apology very likely brought forth to head off threats by gay activists to smother her soon-to-debut TV series, *Dr. Laura*, in its cradle. Said John Aravosis, spokesman for StopDrLaura.com, "If this were Dr. Laura calling her own show, she'd be berated for this apology." The good doctor told columnist Don Feder that the statement was not even an apology but, rather, a clarification. *March 10, 2000*

—

"While I express my opinions from the perspective of an Orthodox Jew and a staunch defender of the traditional family, in talking about gays and lesbians some of my words were poorly chosen. Many people perceive them as hate speech. This fact has been personally and professionally devastating to me as well as to many others . . . On the Day of Atonement, Jews are commanded to seek forgiveness from people we have hurt. I deeply regret the hurt this situation has caused the gay and lesbian community."

Dr. Laura Schlessinger, with her critically lambasted TV show tanking, taking out a back-page ad on Yom Kippur in a special Gay Hollywood issue of *Daily Variety* to reapologize (or to further clarify). *October 11, 2000*

—

"I know in my heart what happened. I know it was an accident and I apologize."

Orlando, FL, DJ Michael Lowe apologizing for unleashing a

stream of profanities in response to a listener's request for
Christmas music, unaware that his microphone was on.
November 29, 1985

—

**"Earlier this week, *All Things Considered* broadcast a
commentary by Andrei Codrescu that described a Christian
pamphlet about the Rapture. Andrei used a vulgar term to
disparage that belief and he said the world would be a better
place without people who hold it. Those remarks offended
listeners and crossed a line of taste and tolerance that we
should have defended with greater vigilance. We spoke with
Andrei who told us that he would like to apologize for what
with hindsight he regards as an inappropriate attempt at
humor. It's one that he regrets and so does NPR."**

National Public Radio spokeswoman Kathy Scott apologizing for contributor Andrei Codrescu's commentary
about life in the aftermath of Christ's resurrection, wherein
"in less than a fifth of a second" four million true believers
ostensibly would disappear from this earthly plane as they
were whisked off to Heaven to hang with Jesus. Said
Codrescu: "The evaporation of four million who believe in
this crap would leave the world an instantly better place."
After NPR's mea culpa, Codrescu explained that he "apologized for the way it was interpreted. I certainly didn't apologize for what I said. Maybe the way I worded it was a bit
strong." *December 22, 1995*

—

**"It is with a heavy heart that I apologize this morning to
Aunt Jemima. She wasn't a self-serving hack politician who**

got up in front of Congress and lied. Aunt Jemima didn't kowtow to Don Rumsfeld or Dick Cheney."

Madison, WI, radio talk host John Sylvester responding to criticism of his comparison of Condoleezza Rice to Aunt Jemima. *November 19, 2004*

———

"We would like to extend a most sincere apology to everyone who was offended by an error in judgment which was not intended to be hurtful or malicious in any way. This was not intended to be a ratings stunt nor was it premeditated. We are truly amazed at how this turned into a media circus and we deeply regret the turmoil that this has caused people all over the country. Beau Duran would like to personally apologize to the following for the unnecessary grief that this media mishap created: Flynn Kile and her family, Tony La Russa and the entire St. Louis Cardinals baseball organization, major league baseball and all the people of St. Louis and Phoenix and all listeners of 98 KUPD."

KUPD in Phoenix apologizing for DJ Beau Duran's making an on-the-air phone call to late Cardinals pitcher Darryl Kile's four-month widow, Flynn, in which he told her how "hot" she was and asked if she had a date to that day's Cardinals versus Diamondbacks playoff game, which led her to hang up and call St. Louis manager La Russa, whose lust for revenge on Duran—"He needs to suffer"—was barely satisfied by the one-week suspension the DJ received. *October 4, 2002*

———

"I shouldn't have said something that I said. I'm sorry. I'll
never say it again."

Washington, D.C., DJ Gary Spears apologizing for his intro-
duction to the Bangles' "Walk Like an Egyptian": "I'm walking
like an Egyptian and smelling like an Arab." *January 30,
1987*

—

"I have become so numb to the horrific things that happen
in this world that I sometimes forget there are still people
who feel. I in no way meant to be insensitive to anyone. My
comments on this were inapropriate [*sic*]."

Marconi, of the newly fired Portland, Oregon, morning shock
jock team Marconi and Tiny, apologizing on his Web site for
playing a tape of the beheading of Nick Berg in Iraq and
laughing about it. *May 14, 2004*

—

"I would certainly apologize for any interpretation of my
words which would appear to be racist. I am not a racist. But
then racism is in the eye of the beholder, not in the heart of
the speaker."

Rochester, New York, talk radio host Bob Lonsberry (a white
Republican) apologizing after being suspended for referring
to the city's mayor, William Johnson Jr. (a black Democrat), as
an orangutan and playing monkey sounds when discussing
him. *September 22, 2003*

—

"I apologize to all who have been offended by my poor decision to go along with playing that insulting (to say the least)

tsunami song. I should have known better and I didn't. So I'm sorry and hopefully we can move forward from this, or I can move forward from this being a better hostess, because I am better than that, and I know better than that—and you deserve better radio than that."

Tarsha Nicole Jones, host of New York's *Miss Jones in the Morning* show on WQHT, apologizing for the daily sing-along by the show's staff of a "We Are the World" parody making fun of the hundreds of thousands of South Asians (or, as the song put it, "screaming chinks") killed by the tsunami. Sample lines: "So now you're screwed / It's the Tsunami / You better run or kiss your ass away / Go find your mommy / I just saw her float by / A tree went through her head / And now the children will be sold to child slavery" and "You can hear God laughing, 'Swim, you bitches, swim.'" Said John C. Liu, a Democratic Asian American councilman from Queens, "This is a piece of garbage. This is degrading to the more than 200,000 people that perished in this disaster. It's insulting to the thousands of New Yorkers and people around the world engaged in relief efforts, and it's just offensive to all of humankind." *January 25, 2005*

———

"I'm truly sorry for the pain and hurt I have caused with my unfeeling comment. I have no excuse for my remark, and regret it. If I could take it back I would. In the course of my show, split second judgment is made over ad-libs. This remark was a grave error in my judgment."

Washington, D.C., shock jock Doug "the Greaseman" Tracht, who thirteen years earlier got himself in trouble by making a tasteless joke about the Martin Luther King Jr. holiday, apologizing for making a tasteless joke about the Texas car-dragging murder of James Byrd Jr.: he played part of a Lauryn Hill song and said, "No wonder people drag them behind trucks." CBS-owned WARW fired him and a contrition tour followed, but it was a year before he landed another gig—at a station in the Virgin Islands, where protests by the largely black audience ended it before it started. Another year of enforced penance followed and then he was back on the air in D.C., albeit on a five-thousand-watt AM outlet whose airtime he had to pay for. *February 25, 1999*

Readin', Writin' & Regrets

"Mr. and Mrs. Brown would like everyone—the school, the community, and the two young men involved in this case—to know that they greatly regret all that has happened. They at no time ever intended for anyone to be hurt, and they apologize for any hurt that has been done to anyone. They want everyone to know that the two young men are not to be blamed for anything. They have done nothing wrong."

Steve Harmon, defense attorney for former Hemet (CA) High School football coach Randy Brown and his wife, Kelly, delivering their apologies after they pleaded guilty (in order to spare their four children the spectacle of a trial) to his having arranged for a seventeen-year-old player on his team to perform oral sex on her (which prosecutors say the player did "well over 100" times). In an interview given by Kelly Brown months earlier, she had said, "When we first got married, we figured we could either be involved together or live two separate lives . . . I really enjoy it. I love football," and said of his players that her husband was "teaching them more than just football. We try to give them a sense of family." *May 28, 1993*

"It was inexcusable. I am sorry for acting like a complete and utter jerk. No, I'm certainly not applauding the slaughter of thousands of innocent people."

University of New Mexico history professor Richard Berthold apologizing for telling his students on September 11, "Anyone who can blow up the Pentagon has my vote." Though his initial position was that "academic freedom and expression" protected his right to say callous and moronic things, a year of retribution by university administrators led to his early retirement. *September 21, 2001*

—

"We have investigated the incident involving your child and others . . . and offer our sincere apologies to you and your child. As a school district, we do not condone the behavior exhibited by the substitute teacher and her services are no longer being used."

Prince George's County School Superintendent Iris T. Metts apologizing in a letter to the families of fifteen Maryland sixth graders whose mouths were covered with folded paper towels and taped shut by substitute teacher Caprisha Boseman, who became upset when they collectively spurned her entreaties to cease talking. *May 26, 2000*

—

"We now understand that the events in question were done in poor taste. The decorations in question contained expressions that do not reflect the opinions of any member of this living unit. We are very, very sorry. We feel great remorse because of this."

Jay Hoffman, president of the all-white Alpha Tau Omega fraternity at Indiana's DePauw University, apologizing for throwing a "ghetto party," which featured racist graffiti written all over the frat house and guests in blackface or decked out as pimps or whores. *October 17, 1988*

—

"Despite reports to the contrary, I did not say, nor do I believe, that girls are intellectually less able than boys, or that women lack the ability to succeed at the highest levels of science . . . I deeply regret the impact of my comments and apologize for not having weighed them more carefully . . . I was wrong to have spoken in a way that was an unintended signal of discouragement to talented girls and women."

Harvard president Lawrence Summers on the university's Web site, embarking on a weeks-long series of mea culpas for a speech in which he mentioned existing research suggesting that women may be innately less gifted than men are in math and science. *January 19, 2005*

—

"I'm here today to issue an apology, first of all, to the Muslim and Buddhist communities. Second, I would like to apologize to the Christian community."

South Carolina Board of Education member Dr. Henry Jordan apologizing for responding, when his suggestion that the Ten Commandments be posted in public schools was rejected because people of other faiths could be offended, "Screw the Buddhists and kill the Muslims." *May 21, 1997*

—

"I did not view it as racial. I wanted to teach the children about prejudice. I did not do it with malice or to embarrass anyone."

Mary Horning, a white first grade teacher at Octorara Elementary in Pennsylvania, apologizing for having the only two black kids in her class portray slaves on an auction block during a history lesson. "Teacher put us up on a table. Acted like she was selling us," said Ashley Dixon (who was told she would have fetched ten dollars at the auction) while Zachary Thomas had to remove his shirt to show how slaves were chained to a post before being flogged. *January 20, 1993*

⸻

"We are painfully aware of the way this incident has been perceived by a large number of people. It was in no way our intention to symbolically represent anything derogatory toward any person or group of people."

Lee D. Tatum, president of the Phi Delta Theta chapter at Kentucky's Centre College, apologizing for a mock hanging in which a fraternity member in blackface swung from a rope while several students wearing robes and carrying torches gathered around the tree beneath him. *November 18, 1988*

⸻

"*The Lariat* has had a tremendously valuable educational experience and is genuinely sorry for any pain that was caused."

The editors of the newspaper of Saddleback Community College in Orange County, CA, apologizing for student

Michael S. Boren's editorial in which he wrote that if the Israelis "are indeed God's chosen people . . . it would seem that God might have made a better choice." *December 19, 1989*

—

"We are disappointed with ourselves that, in attempting to measure anti-Arabic prejudice among non-Arabic students at Dearborn High School, we inadvertently insulted those whose problems . . . we were attempting to expose, deal with and rectify."

Dearborn (MI) High School principal Ann Superko apologizing for a survey intended to determine students' attitudes toward Arab Americans—a survey whose questions about Arabs (Do they deal drugs? Do they pay their fair share of taxes? Do they have poor hygiene habits?) created among students tensions that hadn't previously existed. *March 19, 1990*

—

"I didn't think anything like this would happen. I seriously thought that just people here on campus would read it . . . If she was offended by it, I apologize."

University of California, Berkeley, political science major Guy Branum apologizing for a column in the student newspaper in which he revealed which dorm Chelsea Clinton lived in at Stanford University and urged readers to "show your spirit on Chelsea's bloodied carcass." Asked Berkeley student Rob Alschuler, "What's wrong with printing where she lives? Isn't that just freedom of the press? Isn't that the . . . whatever amendment?" *November 21, 1997*

—

"If anybody was offended, that was not my intent and I have apologized."

Dr. Richard Stock, gynecology professor at the University of Pittsburgh, apologizing for cartoons he included in his lecture that portrayed female sex organs as meat in a butcher shop. *May 10, 1989*

—

"I think what I did was stupid. I hope it was temporary stupidity and not terminal."

Ted Simonson, principal of Los Gatos High School in California, apologizing for saying, "I understand they are going to change the name of the Bay Bridge to the Walt Disney Bridge because it connects Fairyland [San Francisco] to Jungleland [Oakland]" and for calling female joggers "jigglers." *January 30, 1992*

—

"I'm very sorry about that happening. We should not be typecasting people, and that was not my intent."

Boston School Committee member Joseph Casper apologizing for saying to a Hispanic candidate for the school superintendency, "You are well dressed, very articulate. You're about as much Hispanic as I am. You are not the traditional Hispanic. You're very smooth." *July 25, 1985*

—

"In retrospect, the letter was a poor attempt at humor. We apologize for the letter and sincerely regret any offense given or taken."

Timothy J. Keating, president of Harvard University's exclusive Pi Eta men's club, apologizing in a letter to the dean for a party invitation in which women were referred to as "fat loads," "meaty but grateful heifers," and "slobbering bovines fresh for the slaughter." *April 13, 1984*

===

"The tumultuous events of the summer have been all-consuming and deeply painful for me, my family, and many members of the Mount Holyoke community. I am solely responsible and wish to express my personal regret to all students, faculty, and administrators who have been affected . . . I am truly sorry for the hurt I have caused."

Pulitzer Prize–winning history professor Joseph J. Ellis, suspended for a year by the Massachusetts college, apologizing for having long claimed to have been a platoon leader and paratrooper in Vietnam when he'd actually avoided active duty by spending four years in grad school. *August 17, 2001*

===

"I explained to them that out of frustration, people will say things in a confidential meeting under stress that they don't mean, and that I apologize to them if it was any way hurtful or offensive to them, and that I would try to be more careful in the future."

David Simmons, athletic director of Washington, D.C.'s Howard University, reporting his apology to the female members of the cheerleading team for saying, when he was asked if he'd be bringing them to a big game in St. Louis, "Those bitches aren't going anywhere." *April 11, 1994*

===

"We have every confidence that this scholarly series would have been presented in a fair and sensitive manner.

Unfortunately, [the language in the promotional flyer] does not describe the series fully and accurately."

New York's American Museum of Natural History apologizing for canceling a lecture series that was to examine the evils of ethnic stereotyping because the brochure promoting the event was itself awash in stereotypes. Among them: Italians evoked "San Genero, the Godfather and the Black Hand, the importance of garlic"; the Chinese amounted to "The dragon, New Year, laundries, restaurants, Confucius, gangs"; and Indians (from India) were summed up as "Festival of Lights, the Sacred Cow, newspaper stands, saris and suits." *February 21, 1986*

═

"I made some inappropriate remarks. If you took offense at anything I said, please accept my apology. I have nothing but the highest esteem for teachers and the teaching profession."

Education Secretary Rod Paige apologizing for referring to the National Education Association, America's largest teachers' union—which was critical of several provisions in the No Child Left Behind law—as a "terrorist organization." *March 1, 2004*

═

"Be it resolved that the Board of Regents agrees that Ward Churchill's post 9/11 comments have brought dishonor to the University . . . Be it further resolved that the Board of Regents apologizes to all Americans, especially those targeted in the 9/11 attacks and those serving in our armed forces, for the disgraceful comments of Professor Churchill."

The University of Colorado Board of Regents in a unanimously approved resolution apologizing for a series of contentious observations by the professor of ethnic studies, among them a reference in a written essay to the World Trade Center victims as "little Eichmanns" because of their labors in the financial industry ("Well, really, let's get a grip, shall we? True enough they were civilians of a sort. But innocent, gimme a break") and the suggestion to an interviewer that, because of the ineffectiveness of protest on U.S. policy in Iraq, "it may be that more 9/11s are necessary." *February 3, 2005*

—

"I was trying to find a shorthand way to explain his incredible effectiveness in dealing with the white institutions. What I did was say a bad thing about someone who has treated me with consideration and friendship. I have to seek forgiveness."

University of Florida president John Lombardi apologizing for referring to Adam Herbert, the incoming black chancellor of the state university system, as an "Oreo." *January 13, 1998*

—

"To family and friends and all others who respect and admire Dr. Martin Luther King Jr., our sincere regrets and profound apologies."

Dr. Robert L. Summitt, dean of the University of Tennessee, Memphis's Center for Health Sciences, apologizing to Coretta Scott King for the use, in a class on gunshot wounds, of autopsy photos showing her husband with his lower jaw and part of his neck blown away by a bullet from a high-powered rifle. *May 10, 1985*

—

"This is an apology to the families and to society in general. We're saying sorry to them all."

David Skorton, vice president for research at the University of Iowa, apologizing for the "regrettable" experiments conducted by the school's speech pathology department at a Davenport orphanage in the late 1930s. As if having no parents was not handicap enough, the kids in the study were subjected to various psychological pressures to induce stuttering—an affliction which, for some of these formerly normal-speaking children, lasted for years, wreaking lifelong havoc on their self-esteem. *June 13, 1981*

—

"I apologize to Mr. and Mrs. Prevette and Johnathan for the misunderstanding that the sexual harassment policy was applied in this matter."

Lexington (NC) school superintendent Jim Simeon apologizing in a hand-delivered letter for the punishment meted out to a Southwest Elementary School first grader—he was made to miss an ice-cream party—for kissing a classmate on her cheek, which apparently violated school policy against "unwarranted and unwelcome touching of one student by another," though Johnathan said the girl asked for the kiss. Said Johnathan's mother, "I don't call this an apology. It's a letter with a bunch of crap about how we misunderstood." *October 4, 1996*

—

"I am here to tell you that I misjudged the situation, and I want to apologize for that. I want you to know today that I will recommend . . . that the word 'evolution' be put back in the curriculum."

Georgia superintendent of schools Kathy Cox apologizing for removing the highly charged word from the proposed science curriculum in the hope of flying under the radar of rabid creationists. *February 5, 2004*

—

"I know my remarks were wrong, damaging and hurtful . . . Racial insensitivity is wrong. No excuses."

Michael F. Musante, Student Association president of Washington, D.C.'s George Washington University, resigning his position while apologizing for saying of his opponent in the election, "Could you imagine if that nigger had won?" *October 29, 1992*

—

"I must admit that some of the language in the tapes is language that I might have used and have used in the past in private situations. I grew up in a different era, and people said things then that are not acceptable today. Obviously I need to work on my language."

Dallas school board member Dan Peavy apologizing after a tape was released of several of his phone conversations in which he referred to "ignorant motherfucking niggers," "damned niggers," "all those niggers," "some nigger," "nigger rights," "the fucking nigger," and "these motherfucking ignorant goddamned little niggers" who attend "these fucking schools." His resignation, unsurprisingly, came within a week. *September 29, 1995*

———

"I just wanted to apologize to you guys for any crap. To everyone I love, I'm really sorry about all this. I know my mom and dad will be just fucking shocked beyond belief."

Colorado high school senior Eric Harris apologizing for being about to go with his friend Dylan Klebold to slaughter students at Columbine High School. *April 20, 1999*

———

"We're sorry there has been so much hurt. It certainly was never intentional. It was a little fifth-grade boy who wrote a report himself, and none of us realized the impact it would have on some people. We're trying to work on it now, to mend some feelings."

Linda Spellman, principal of Westlake (CA) Elementary School, apologizing for allowing a student to dress up as Adolf Hitler and deliver a first-person speech that attempted to provide some context for the Nazi leader's genocidal tendencies. "My mother died of cancer while being treated by a Jewish doctor," the boy—wearing a swastika armband and fake mustache—said, adding that when he enrolled at an arts academy in Vienna, the headmaster "thought my drawings were TERRIBLE! . . . Later I learned that the headmaster was Jewish." *February 28, 1992*

The Boob Tube

"I had not intended that our actions cause anyone harm, and I hereby apologize . . . to the public in general for such action."

Psychic Tamara Rand apologizing for claiming that a Las Vegas talk show appearance in which she uncannily predicted details of the assassination attempt on President Ronald Reagan—that there would be "gunshots" and a "thud" in Reagan's chest, that the attack would occur during "the last few days of March," that it would be carried out by a fair-haired young man named "Jack Humley"—was taped in early January, when it was actually taped the day after the shooting. *April 5, 1981*

—

"I just want to apologize to Sharon Gless and her family and any of her friends for all the stress and trouble I've caused. I want her to feel safe, because she is from me, and I'm really sorry for what I did."

Obsessed fan Joni Leigh Penn apologizing for breaking into the *Cagney and Lacey* star's home with an assault rifle, with which she'd intended to kill herself after sexually assaulting Gless, who wasn't home at the time. *July 16, 1990*

—

"I am sincerely sorry that I've scared people. I will never let this happen again."

Australian wildlife expert Steve Irwin apologizing on NBC's *Today Show* for feeding a dead chicken to a thirteen-foot crocodile with one hand while holding his one-month-old son in his other arm. *January 5, 2004*

—

"I feel terrible about it, and I deeply apologize to anyone I might have offended."

Democratic National Convention producer Don Mischer apologizing for freaking out on the air over yet another failed Democratic balloon drop. "Go balloons. I don't see anything happening. Jesus, we need more balloons," he said, unaware he was being broadcast around the world. "I want all balloons to go. Goddamn. No confetti. No confetti. No confetti. I want more balloons. What's happening to the balloons? All balloons—where the hell—there's nothing falling. What the fuck are you guys doing up there?" *July 30, 2004*

—

"Though my comments were said in jest and not intended for publication, I realize I have made a terrible mistake for which I am truly sorry."

Craig Kilborn, the host of Comedy Central's *The Daily Show* back when it didn't win Emmys, apologizing for his assessment to an *Esquire* writer of his difficult working relationship with the show's cocreator and head writer Lizz Winstead: "There are a lot of bitches on the staff, and, hey, they're emotional people. You can print that! You know how women are—they overreact. It's not really a big deal. And to be honest, Lizz does find me very attractive. If I wanted her to blow me, she would." Kilborn failed to explain how a comment accompanied by the exclamation, "You can print that!" was "not intended for publication." *December 15, 1997*

—

"This graphic—which was not accompanied by any remarks from Craig Kilborn—should not have been included in the telecast and is not consistent with our broadcast standards. CBS and Worldwide Pants Inc . . . deeply regret this incident."

The network and production company responsible for *The Late Late Show* apologizing for the appearance of a graphic that read "Snipers Wanted" over the image of George W. Bush. *August 9, 2000*

—

"We were trying to be a little humorous and irreverent. We apologize."

Court TV marketing executive Dan Levinson apologizing for his network's "Wives with Knives" promotion, which featured a mightily pissed-off wife reaching for a steak knife with the clear intention of carving up her Super Bowl–watching husband as a voice-over said, "Don't get angry, ladies, get even. Watch 'Wives with Knives.' . . . Five riveting hours, five emotional stories of real women who went after their husbands." *January 29, 1999*

—

"I'm sorry I didn't sing so good. I'd like to hear him sing it."
Comedian Roseanne Barr responding to President George Bush's assessment of her cacophonous singing of the national anthem (and subsequent spitting and crotch grabbing) in front of booing San Diego Padres fans as "disgraceful." Despite her use of the word "sorry," Barr insisted, "I'm not going to apologize for doing it" (though she did acknowledge, "I probably should have waited a while before I scratched myself and spit"). *July 27, 1990*

=

"I unequivocally apologize and have apologized if I've offended anyone."
Roseanne Barr, after three more days of national tumult, apologizing on *The Sally Jessy Raphaël Show*. *July 30, 1990*

=

"It got on the air by mistake. We apologize to our viewers."
Fred DeMarco, VP and general manager of WRC in Washington, D.C., apologizing for a promo in between *Punky Brewster* and *Silver Spoons* for an upcoming local news story about a computer bulletin board system used "by adult men to exchange hard-core stories about sex with teen-aged boys . . . 'High Tech Sex' is a story that could affect any home with a computer." *February 24, 1986*

=

"We have heard from many of our viewers about last night's *MNF* opening segment and we agree that the placement was inappropriate. We apologize."
ABC apologizing for opening its *Monday Night Football*

broadcast with a filmed segment in which *Desperate House-wives* star Nicollette Sheridan turned up in an empty locker room wearing nothing but a towel, which she then dropped in an effort to seduce Philadelphia Eagles wide receiver Terrell Owens, into whose arms she then nakedly jumped. *November 16, 2004*

"We are very sorry if anyone was offended."
CBS spokeswoman Nancy Carr apologizing to Native Americans for OutKast's feathers-and-war-paint costumes during their Grammy Awards performance of "Hey Ya!" *February 13, 2004*

"I make no excuses. I was wrong and what I said was hurtful to people and I feel terrible about it."
Politically Incorrect host Bill Maher apologizing for comparing his dogs to "retarded children" and then, when one of his guests said she had a nine-year-old retarded nephew whom she'd never thought of like a dog, telling her, "Well, maybe you should." *January 17, 2001*

"Kathie or I had no knowledge of this. We just want to change things. She is sick about it. I am very sorry, and I apologize for our country. God bless all of you."
Ex–football-star Frank Gifford doing damage control after it turned out that his wife Kathie Lee's clothing line was manufactured not only in Honduran sweatshops but in a New York one as well, apologizing as he delivered three hundred

dollars each to thirty underpaid workers who slaved away for less than minimum wage in Manhattan. And, of course, self-obsessed Kathie Lee saw herself as the real victim here. *May 23, 1996*

—

"At the end of this past week's telecast of *Saturday Night Live*, a member of the regular cast ad-libbed live a gutter term, which we would, of course, never allow on an NBC program. We deeply regret this incident and are taking the appropriate action to preclude its re-occurrence."

NBC responding to sixty-one complaints from viewers by apologizing for Charles Rocket's having said "Fuck" on the air during a sketch. *February 23, 1981*

—

"This song is in fact a parody of the opening numbers of countless Broadway musicals which are designed to set the scene for the story that follows. We regret that the song taken out of context has caused offense."

Fox Network president Jamie Kellner apologizing for a song featured on *The Simpsons* (in the episode "A Streetcar Named Marge") that called New Orleans "crummy, lousy, rancid, and rank." *October 2, 1992*

—

"MTV apologizes for his breach of his agreement with us and we apologize to our viewers."

MTV VP Barry Kluger apologizing for comedian Andrew Dice Clay's X-rated material on the network's awards show,

and announcing that Clay was banned from MTV for life.
September 6, 1989

—

**"There are times when half statements get misinterpreted,
and that's what happened at the Aspen U.S. Comedy
Festival last week . . . My kids are innocent, and they
deserve your care and goodwill. Please accept my humble
apology, and let's get back to where we were."**

Jerry Lewis, having heard that more than a few telethon
donors were offended by the anti-female-comic stance he
took during a Q&A session, apologizing for saying, "A
woman doing comedy doesn't offend me but sets me back a
bit. I, as a viewer, have trouble with it. I think of her as a
producing machine that brings babies in the world."
Reserving particular contempt for the ones who work dirty,
Lewis explained, "When women, doing comedy, do routines
written for them by drill sergeants, I take objection. Their
filth makes me and many ashamed to be in our business,
and to me women doing anything, especially comedy, are
looked upon by me as one of God's great miracles . . . They
can make a baby . . . I see women as incredibly strong people
who deserve our undying respect." *February 17, 2000*

—

**"It is certainly not how I feel. I admire people with disabili-
ties. That's why I've worked so hard for all these years. Many
of the people that I work closely with are in wheelchairs and
I have never seen any of them as inferior to anyone else.
They are my friends and co-workers. I would never intentionally harm or demean anyone with a disability."**

Jerry Lewis apologizing for saying that pity is the motivating force among telethon donors: "If it's pity, we'll get some money. I'm giving you facts. Pity. You don't want to be pitied because you're a cripple in a wheelchair, stay in your house." *June 1, 2001*

⸺

"Last night after the game, those of you who watched our live report from the locker room may have seen more of one player than you expected. If you were offended by that, we apologize. But more important than that, to that player goes our sincerest apology. He was totally unaware we were on the air and he had no idea he would show up in our picture. It was one of those inadvertent things that sometimes happen in a live situation. But that doesn't mean we regret it any less."

WJLA sports director Frank Herzog apologizing for his station's having broadcast several seconds of Washington Redskins defensive tackle Tim Johnson naked. *September 10, 1991*

⸺

"At the conclusion of our 10 o'clock newscast last night, I attributed statements to Chicago Bears quarterback Jim McMahon. McMahon and the Chicago Bears have denied these statements and I have no reason to doubt their denials. I sincerely apologize to Jim McMahon, the Chicago Bears, the NFL, Chicago radio station WLS, and to the people of New Orleans for the problems caused by these unverified statements."

Buddy Diliberto, sports director of WDSU-TV in New Orleans, apologizing for telling viewers that he'd heard McMahon had given a Chicago radio interview in which he said, "All the women in New Orleans are sluts and all the men are stupid." Diliberto was suspended by station general manager Bob McRaney Jr., who also apologized, saying, "We have no basis to believe the statements about New Orleans attributed to McMahon were ever made." *January 22, 1986*

—

"If my comments brought pain to anyone I certainly did not intend for this to happen and apologize for any such reaction. I especially appeal to my many listeners in the gay community to accept my apologies for any inadvertent insults which may have occurred."

MSNBC talk show host Michael Savage apologizing for an exchange that got him fired, in which he told a caller, "Oh, you're one of the sodomites. You should only get AIDS and die, you pig." *July 8, 2003*

—

"I said things that ended up hurting Oprah Winfrey's feelings and far too late it was pointed out to me that this was happening. I feel bad for a number of reasons, because I really don't like to hurt people, and I feel bad because the person being hurt is actually a really good person for American writing and reading."

Novelist Jonathan Franzen apologizing for his reaction to his book *The Corrections* being selected by Oprah Winfrey for her book club, which was to worry publicly that the presence on his book's cover of Oprah's seal of approval (or, as he described it, "that logo of corporate ownership")—a pop culture imprimatur guaranteed to greatly increase his sales—would somehow cheapen his highbrow fiction. "She's picked some good books, but she's picked enough schmaltzy, one-dimensional ones that I cringe, myself," said Franzen, whose tortured ambivalence over winning the literary lottery got him disinvited from Oprah's show. The end result of the author's Brobdingnagian ingratitude: a disheartened Oprah discontinued her book club for several years, leading to a significant decline in fiction sales. *October 23, 2001*

"I have apologized to NBC . . . for not informing them about the incident. I had believed it was a private matter that had been resolved."

Rob Campos, the bachelor for whose affections fifteen women were competing on NBC's *For Love or Money*, apologizing for failing to reveal an incident during his days as a Marine in which he barged into the female barracks and drunkenly groped a Navy officer. *June 9, 2003*

"An overly aggressive CBS News producer jumped the gun with a report that should have been offered to local stations for their late news. We sincerely regret the error."

CBS apologizing for cutting off the ending of *CSI:NY* with a report on the death of Yasser Arafat. *November 11, 2004*

"I want to apologize for my comments. Let me assure you they were made in jest with no intention to offend . . . You are a bright shining talent. It was a great achievement that you finished in the top ten. Half the women in America would kill to be in your shoes . . . In this case I'm the 'real dummy.'"

Miss America celebrity judge Larry King apologizing in a telegram (accompanied by a dozen red roses) to Marla Wynne (Miss Pennsylvania) for responding to Joan Rivers's question about who was "the ugliest" contestant by saying unequivocally, "Miss Pennsylvania," and volunteering this review of her talent segment: "She did a great ventriloquist bit . . . The dummy was prettier." Said Wynne's mother, "She is by far not ugly. For him to attack any girl who was on that stage, in his position as a judge, I think, is contemptible." *September 11, 1990*

"We apologize for the joke referencing Miss Colombia . . . There was no intent to offend her or the people of Colombia."

David Letterman and CBS executives apologizing for the host's saying about the Miss Universe pageant, "You know what has really gotten impressive? The talent competition. For example, Miss Colombia, she swallowed fifty balloons full of heroin." *May 15, 2001*

"Mr. Costas did not intend any disrespect to the People's Republic of China or its citizens . . . We apologize for any resulting hurt feelings."

NBC Sports VP Ed Markey apologizing in a letter to Chinese groups offended that sportscaster Bob Costas dared to mention China's human rights problems during the opening ceremonies of the Olympics in Atlanta. "The comments were not based on NBC beliefs," Markey wrote. "Nobody at NBC ever intends to offend anyone." *August 20, 1996*

Judges and Lawyers and Cops, Oh My!

"The comment was not meant to be a regional slur. To the extent that it was misinterpreted to be one, I apologize."

Assistant U.S. Attorney Kenneth Taylor apologizing for referring to potential jurors in the eastern Kentucky mountains as "illiterate cave dwellers." *October 17, 2003*

———

"I am apologizing not only to the Williams family but to the residents of the Mattapan community and the entire city for this tragedy. The one tragic fact which is clear at this time is that Rev. Accelyne Williams was an innocent victim in the continuing war on drugs."

Boston police commissioner Paul Evans apologizing for the death of a seventy-five-year-old retired minister who died of a heart attack shortly after a thirteen-member rifle-bearing SWAT team mistakenly burst into his apartment (instead of the one above his), chased him into his bedroom, and handcuffed him. Said family lawyer John Drewery, "The family is going to be looking for much more than an apology." *March 26, 1994*

———

"Never did I intend to disparage such efforts or to criticize any citizen, organization or government body. Deeply and sincerely, I regret that it appeared so."

Annapolis judge Thomas Curley apologizing for referring to anti-drunk-driving groups as "sanctimonious" after finding a Maryland official innocent of drunk driving and describing efforts to deal with the problem as "the fad of the moment." *November 15, 1983*

—

"Although I didn't intend to offend anyone, obviously I did. I can only hope my apology has been accepted."

Lawyer Scott Mitchell apologizing for playing a tape—for the amusement of fellow attendees of a Florida Bar convention— on which a sexual assault victim described her attack. *July 10, 1991*

—

"There were some people who were offended by [what I said] and more importantly, there were some people who were hurt by it. I deeply regret that."

San Jose, CA, fire chief Robert Osby apologizing for announcing, during a conversation about his department's affirmative action policy, that he was not about to hire people who were "wearing pink shirts and swaying." The apology also covered Osby's having affected a lisp and an effeminate demeanor as he said, "If some guy comes prancing into my office in a pink leisure suit saying, 'I just love truck men,' I'm not going to hire him." *May 5, 1986*

—

"If anyone has been offended, I'm sorry for that."

Los Angeles Police chief Daryl Gates apologizing for telling the *Los Angeles Times* that one possible reason that blacks seemed to be more likely to die from police choke holds—of fifteen such deaths around that time, twelve had been black—was that their carotid arteries "do not open as fast as they do on normal people." *May 11, 1982*

"I made a mistake for which I have suffered in not realizing at the time that the letter could be taken seriously as not a joke. I never thought about it not being taken as a joke because I am not a racist."

Okaloosa County, FL, sheriff's deputy David Murphy apologizing for sending a letter out to hunters advising them that, due to a "shortage of big game animals," they should hunt black people. Murphy's letter of apology, published in the *Fort Walton Beach Playground Daily News*, recounted his 1966 experiences in Vietnam, when he said he was wounded while looking out for inexperienced black soldiers: "I took an interest in their welfare. I wrote letters for them to their parents. I have love, not ill feeling, in my heart for all people." *March 15, 1981*

"I was venting. It was unnecessary, wrong and stupid."

Richard "Deacon" Jones, a county judge in Omaha, apologizing for various instances of bizarre behavior that led to his removal from the bench by the Nebraska Supreme Court. Among them: throwing firecrackers into the office of a colleague he'd sent an anonymous death threat to (which acts he minimized as "pranks that went wrong"), setting absurd bail amounts ("thirteen cents," "a zillion dollars," "a gazillion pengos"), and signing court documents with names not his ("Mickey Mouse," "Snow White," "Adolf Hitler"). *January 21, 1998*

"In retrospect, it was the wrong thing to do and I simply won't make excuses."

San Mateo County, CA, judge George Taylor apologizing for cutting San Francisco Giants slugger Barry Bonds's family support payments in half and then, after the hearing, asking for his autograph. *August 24, 1994*

"It was always my intent to remain true to my vows, but despite my intentions, failures and mistakes happened."

Bedford County, PA, District Justice Charles O. Guyer apologizing (and resigning) for promising special treatment to a defendant in exchange for being allowed to get himself sexually aroused by shampooing the man's hair. *May 5, 1992*

"The remarks were inappropriate. It's something I've never done before and won't do again."

Florida Circuit Judge Gene Stephenson apologizing for looking at a photo of a rape victim during a court hearing and saying, "Why would he want to rape her? She doesn't look like a day at the beach." *January 29, 2004*

"My comments, appearing out of context, are both insulting and sexist."

Philadelphia judge Bernard J. Avellino apologizing to a rape victim whose looks he disparaged to the defendant at a hearing ("This was an unattractive girl and you are a good-looking fellow. You did something to her which was stupid") and in an interview where he referred to the victim as "the ugliest girl I have ever seen in my entire life . . . in the top ten" and called her "coyote ugly." *February 4, 1986*

—

"Having reviewed the transcript of the hearing, I realize that some of my words were not well-chosen and might have conveyed implications which I did not intend. For this I apologize."

Grant County, WI, judge William Reinecke apologizing for referring to a five-year-old girl who was sexually assaulted by her mother's live-in boyfriend as "an unusually sexually promiscuous young lady." *January 23, 1982*

—

"Although my remarks have been taken out of context, I take responsibility for the fact that they have indeed caused heartache. I was wrong and I apologize. I am not a racist."

San Francisco lawyer Melvin Belli apologizing for referring to the "goddamn Chinese" at a Toronto convention and advising attorneys in civil cases to avoid "stingy" Chinese jurors. Confronted by forty Chinese American protesters outside his office, Belli said, "I love the Chinese and every Chinaman in town should know that," prompting a demonstrator to cite his use of the term "Chinaman" as proof of his prejudice. *July 28, 1982*

⸗

"I had one and offered some to two members of the press and then made a remark which was meant to be facetious and was taken by those who received it as being facetious. However, I understand the sensitivities of people and, in hindsight, those remarks could have been misconstrued . . . If any person, or persons, was offended, my sincere and most humble apologies are given."

O. J. Simpson's attorney Robert Shapiro apologizing for celebrating the defense's brutal cross-examination of police criminalist Dennis Fung by giving out fortune cookies and saying, "This is from Hang Fung restaurant." *April 17, 1995*

⸗

"I'm apologizing from the bottom of my heart for creating pain where pain wasn't necessary. I don't know what else to do."

Former Los Angeles detective Mark Fuhrman apologizing to Diane Sawyer on *Primetime Live* for his repeated use—in taped discussions with a would-be screenwriter—of the word "nigger," which he'd denied under oath at the O. J. Simpson trial ever having uttered. *October 8, 1996*

⸗

"I do apologize."

U.S. Capitol police officer C. M. Hazlip apologizing to *U.S. News and World Report* photographer Linda Creighton for pushing her camera into her face to prevent her from taking a picture of key Iran-Contra figure Adm. John Poindexter. *December 2, 1986*

—

"[He] didn't deserve to be whacked around like that, and I'll be the first to apologize to him for that. But he doesn't deserve to be a folk hero either."

Police chief Daryl Gates apologizing for the beating Rodney G. King received at the hands of four Los Angeles cops— Officers Laurence Powell, Timothy Wind, Theodore Briseno and Sergeant Stacey Koon—who didn't know they were being videotaped. *March 6, 1991*

—

"In spite of the fact that he's on parole and a convicted robber, I'd be glad to apologize. He did not deserve that beating. We are ashamed of the fact that he got that beating and no question about it, he deserves an apology or more."

Daryl Gates apologizing again for the Rodney King beating. *March 8, 1991*

—

"We apologize to the members of other departments because we have brought shame and dishonor to the profession. It is a unanimous opinion of this department that that kind of conduct was wrong. It was humiliating."

Daryl Gates apologizing yet again for the Rodney King beating. *March 13, 1991*

—

"If anyone has ever been offended, hurt, or feels hurt from the things I've said, let me just apologize to you and tell you that never have I had the intent to harm anyone, at all."

Daryl Gates expanding the boundaries of his contrition at a
meeting with black leaders. *April 18, 1991*

—

**"I am deeply ashamed and sorry for what I have done to
others—to Mrs. Silverman, to my family, and to those who
entrusted New York's court system to my care."**

Former New York chief judge Sol Wachtler apologizing for a
fourteen-month campaign of harassing letters and phone
calls to his former lover Joy Silverman (including the threat to
kidnap her daughter), all of which were meant to frighten her
into resuming their relationship. *March 31, 1993*

—

**"I regret sincerely the pain my comments caused last week,
particularly to survivors of the Holocaust. The horrors of the
Holocaust were unique in the annals of human history."**

Montreal Superior Court Justice Jean Bienvenue apologizing
for comparing the way the Nazis dispatched their victims in
concentration camps favorably with the violence a defendant
used to murder her husband. "The Nazis did not eliminate
millions of Jews in a painful and bloody manner," he
explained. "They died in gas chambers without suffering."
December 12, 1995

—

**"I am truly sorry and apologize profusely for the episode and
most particularly for any embarrassment my remarks may
have caused you, my colleagues, and the court."**

New York Federal Appeals Court Judge Guido Calabresi
apologizing to Chief Judge John Walker for pointing out in a

speech that George W. Bush's rise to power followed the same path as those of Hitler and Mussolini in that, just as "Hindenburg put Hitler in" and "Mussolini was put in by the king of Italy," here "the Supreme Court . . . in *Bush v. Gore* . . . put somebody in power." While insisting that he was not taking a partisan position—even as he said that "the structural reassertion of democracy" demanded that voters oust Bush in 2004—he also took pains to emphasize that he was "not suggesting for a moment that Bush is Hitler . . . but it is a situation which is extremely unusual." *June 24, 2004*

—

"Anytime a situation occurs where there is a leak and it subjects a person to such public focus, I'm sorry it happened."

U.S. Attorney General Janet Reno finally offering up the merest grunt of an apology to Richard Jewell, who went from anonymous schlub to hero (he was the security guard who spotted the knapsack containing the pipe bomb at the Atlanta Olympics) to villain (thanks to an FBI or Justice Department leak, he quickly became the assumed-guilty prime suspect in that bombing) to national punch line (as the doofus whose life was ruined by being publicly suspected—no matter how wrongly—of a famous crime). *July 31, 1997*

—

"I regret making these statements. I made a mistake in making statements that could have been considered by the court to be a breach of the court's order. And for that I apologize to the court and counsel."

U.S. Attorney General John Ashcroft apologizing for twice

violating a gag order in connection with a Detroit terrorism case, first by suggesting that the defendants knew in advance about the 9/11 attacks, and then by praising a key government witness during the trial. *December 16, 2003*

—

"I have made a mistake, I was wrong, I did not adequately perceive the significance of the matter. Quite honestly, I was acting at that moment more as a mother than as a person who would be sitting here before you to be attorney general."

U.S. Attorney General–designate Zoë Baird apologizing at her confirmation hearing for hiring illegal aliens as household help and paying them off the books. She withdrew from consideration for the post within days. *January 19, 1993*

—

"I owe an enormous apology to the president for whatever distraction this may have caused. This is my responsibility. This is my mistake."

Former New York police commissioner Bernard Kerik, nominated to head the Department of Homeland Security, apologizing for having to withdraw his name from consideration because he failed to inform White House officials about the housekeeper whose salary he hadn't paid the required taxes on, and who might not even be in this country legally. *December 11, 2004*

—

"I want to apologize to this community for the remarks made by members of this department. Our training officers

made statements that certain ethnic groups may be less susceptible to the effects of pepper spray. There is no empirical or scientific evidence to support these statements."

Cambridge, MA, police commissioner Ronnie Watson apologizing for training officer Frank Gutoski's observation that pepper spray is often ineffective against "people who have consumed cayenne pepper from the time they are small children, and this generally breaks into ethnic categories"—i.e., Mexican Americans. *August 13, 1999*

"I apologize for and regret my recent statements which partially provided examples of situations which may arise in considering the issue of a waiver of parental consent in proceedings brought under the new Parental Rights Restoration Act. Contrary to the way in which my remarks have been construed, I believe that the race of the victim and the race of the perpetrator of a rape have no bearing on the reprehensibleness of the crime."

Mason County, MI, Probate Court Judge Francis K. Bourisseau apologizing for saying that he would not allow minors to receive abortions without parental consent except for situations where a white girl was raped by a black man. *May 2, 1991*

"I want to apologize for a poor choice of words describing the victims of the Bednarski case. I did not mean to condemn the homosexual community generally and I used a poor choice of words and I'm sorry about that . . . I did not intend to state that any victim of crime was entitled to less fair treatment."

Texas state District Judge Jack Hampton apologizing for telling the *Dallas Times Herald* that he gave a killer a lesser sentence in part because his two victims were gay. Explained Hampton, "These two guys that got killed wouldn't have been killed if they hadn't been cruising the streets picking up teenage boys. I don't much care for queers cruising the streets picking up teenage boys. I've got a teenage boy." *December 22, 1988*

"I deeply regret the ungentlemanly tone of those remarks. The comments represented six years of frustration in being the only trial court in the commonwealth without an administrative staff and an ever-increasing workload. Nevertheless, there can be no justification for such unbecoming comments. I offer my apologies to all parties."

E. George Daher, chief justice of Boston Housing Court, apologizing for calling Massachusetts senate president William Bulger a "corrupt midget." *May 12, 1987*

"The first thing I'd like to do is apologize to each and every police officer that has had to work under the guise I left them two years ago. It's a very difficult job and I made it much more difficult, and for that I apologize."

Former New York City police officer Michael Dowd apologizing as he received a fourteen-year prison sentence for cocaine-related activities (including, once, snorting it off the hood of his police car) that, when discovered, led to a department-wide investigation into police corruption. *July 11, 1994*

"If my celebration of the return of fugitive Billy Wayne Williams offended any member of the community, I deeply apologize."

Dallas District Judge Faith Johnson apologizing for celebrating the return of a recaptured defendant with a courtroom party complete with balloons and cake. *May 12, 2005*

—

"My perception of problems needing improvement, and my impatience in addressing them, produced an unacceptable attitude and demeanor which have harmed our system more than improved it."

Franklin County, OH, judge William Millard apologizing as he faced suspension for reacting to a witness being twenty minutes late by dismissing a child rape case. *November 26, 1993*

—

"I regret the jokes which I used . . . [and] I apologize to those who were present. I assure you that there would be no further use of such jokes."

Armando Rodriguez, a member of the Equal Employment Opportunity Commission, apologizing for telling several inappropriate stories (among them, one about a Mexican American woman who mixes up the terms "check up" and "shack up" and another one about female sex organs and the cleanliness thereof) to a decidedly unamused audience during a speech to the Federal Bar Association of Denver. Rodriguez explained that the jokes, described by an attendee of the luncheon as "inexcusable, utterly disgraceful," were supposed to be examples of the "language confusion" endemic to people of different cultures. *February 21, 1980*

⸻

"I wish to again express my apologies to those who have been impacted by my inappropriate conduct."

New Hampshire judge Franklin Jones apologizing in his resignation letter for groping five women at a conference focusing on sexual assault. *January 26, 2005*

⸻

"[This is] conduct which is not consistent with the policies and procedures of the Los Angeles Police Department. The department regrets that these arrests occurred."

Los Angeles Police chief Daryl Gates apologizing to Rabbi Shlomo Cunin and twelve of his students for the verbal and physical abuse they suffered while being arrested by nightstick-wielding cops for disturbing the peace after someone complained that they were praying too loudly in their school. Cunin said that he blacked out as a result of a police choke hold and that the group was subjected to a stream of anti-Semitic invective, culminating in this greeting by an officer at the station: "We have ovens waiting for you." *February 24, 1981*

⸻

"I apologize to those that were offended by my comments. I understand how inappropriate and unacceptable they were."

Charles W. Williams, chief of police in Marshall, TX, and an appointee of Gov. George W. Bush to lead the state's Commission on Law Enforcement Officers Standards and Education, apologizing for several comments he made while being deposed in a 1998 racial discrimination lawsuit filed against him and his department. Asked about various terms alleged to have been used by him or his officers, Williams had explained that he didn't consider pejoratives like "black bastard" or "porch monkey" to be racial slurs and said that as recently as fifty years ago blacks didn't mind at all being called "niggers." Bush claimed to have known nothing of these comments when he named Williams to the commission, from which he resigned days later with further expressions of regret for "not making my points clearer to everyone concerned." *April 7, 2000*

Slinking Off the Silver Screen

"This is possibly the most shameful situation I've ever gotten myself in in my life, and I've done some pretty dumb things in my life. So to actually make a new number one is spectacularly stupid . . . Hopefully at some stage, I'll be able to apologize directly to Nestor but at the moment, he's not answering his phone."

Actor Russell Crowe apologizing on David Letterman's show for angrily throwing a malfunctioning phone in New York's Mercer Hotel and striking concierge Nestor Estrada in the face. *June 8, 2005*

"It's embarrassing and it's wrong and we will take appropriate action. We put an end to it immediately."

Sony spokeswoman Susan Tick apologizing for the studio's fabricating a film critic named David Manning (supposedly from the *Ridgefield Press* in Connecticut) and running his made-up blurbs in ads for four Sony films: *The Animal* ("The producing team of *Big Daddy* has delivered another winner!"), *A Knight's Tale* (actor Heath Ledger is "this year's hottest new star!"), *Vertical Limit* ("Stupendous!"), and *Hollow Man* ("One hell of a scary ride!"). Then two weeks later Tick had to admit that two Sony employees were among

the moviegoers providing man-in-the-street testimonials in a
TV spot for the Mel Gibson film *The Patriot* ("A perfect date
movie!"), which Tick dismissed as an "isolated incident that
occurred a year ago." *June 5, 2001*

—

"The Academy sincerely apologizes to Disney for the unauthorized use of Disney's Snow White character and for
unintentionally creating the impression that Disney had
participated in or sanctioned the opening production
number on the Academy Awards telecast. We pride
ourselves on our meticulousness in obtaining the proper
legal clearances for all music, film and other material used
on our show and regret that we didn't do it with Disney. As
copyright owners ourselves, we have a keen appreciation of
such matters."

Motion Picture Academy president Richard Kahn apologizing for the Allan Carr–produced show's appropriating a
character it didn't own for a seemingly endless opening
number, though not expressing any remorse for the other-
worldly awfulness of the performance itself. *April 6, 1989*

—

"Taken in context, what I was saying was that, compared to
Europe, America is a very young country and we are still
growing as a nation. It is a shame that the metaphor I used
was taken so radically out of context and slung about irre-
sponsibly by the news media. There was no anti-Amer-
ican sentiment. In fact, it was just the opposite. I am an
American. I love my country and have great hopes for it. It
is for this reason that I speak candidly and sometimes

**critically about it. I have benefited greatly from the freedom
that exists in my country and for this I am eternally grateful."**

Actor Johnny Depp apologizing for describing America as "a
dumb puppy that has big teeth that can bite and hurt you" in
an interview with the German magazine *Stern*, where he also
talked about his reaction to the effort by two Republican
congressmen to rename french fries as "freedom fries" in the
House cafeteria: "I was ecstatic because they revealed themselves as idiots." *September 4, 2003*

***

**"It was not my intention to harm, insult or in any way demean
the Jewish people or persons with AIDS."**

Game show host Bob Eubanks apologizing for telling an
offensive joke to the crew of Michael Moore's *Roger and
Me*—"Why do Jewish women never get AIDS? They only
marry assholes, they don't screw 'em"—unaware that the
cameras were rolling and Moore would include it in his film.
December 20, 1989

***

**"I was trying to help end the killing. But there were times I
was thoughtless and careless about it and I'm . . . very sorry
that I hurt them. And I want to apologize to them and to their
families."**

Actress Jane Fonda on ABC's *20/20*, apologizing to Vietnam
War veterans for her visit to Hanoi in 1972, and specifically
for posing for pictures behind a North Vietnamese antiair-
craft gun. "I'm in the communication business. I know the
power of images," she told Barbara Walters. "To have put
myself in a situation like that was a thoughtless and cruel

thing to have done . . . I take full responsibility for it. I was not a kid, you know. The responsibility is mine." At their convention two months later, the unimpressed Veterans of Foreign Wars passed a unanimous resolution demanding that she "be tried by the United States government as a traitor." *June 17, 1988*

—

"I wanna apologize to the gay people—I've never really apologized. And to anyone else who's been offended by any kind of thing that I've done."
Comedian Eddie Murphy apologizing, in a *Parade* magazine interview, to homosexuals for joking about AIDS, and to Lucille Ball, Jackie Gleason, and Red Skelton for using language they'd publicly declared their disapproval of. *February 24, 1985*

—

"Following the reports in today's papers, I just want to say I am deeply ashamed and upset that I've hurt Sienna and the people most close to us. I want to publicly apologize to Sienna and our respective families for the pain that I have caused. There is no defense for my actions, which I sincerely regret."
British actor Jude Law apologizing for cheating on fiancé Sienna Miller with his kid's nanny. *July 18, 2005*

—

"Last night I did something completely insane. I have hurt people I love and embarrassed people I work with. For both things, I am more sorry than I can ever possibly say."

British actor Hugh Grant—who, remember, was living with
Estée Lauder model Elizabeth Hurley at the time—apologizing for getting arrested in his car in Hollywood while
being fellated by prostitute Divine Brown. Grant's contrition
was immortalized on *The Tonight Show with Jay Leno*,
where his appearance at the height of the media monsoon
was credited with starting Leno's resurgence in his ratings
battle against CBS's David Letterman. Grant, whose film
*The Englishman Who Went Up a Hill but Came Down a
Mountain* had recently opened, was described by movie
producer Stuart Cornfeld as "The Englishman who went up
a side street and came down a whore's throat." *June 27, 1995*

In the Penalty Box

"I want to make it clear to everyone and especially to our young people that prejudice and bigotry are hurtful, hateful, unacceptable and demeaning to all people . . . If I have said anything to offend anyone, it was never my intention and I apologize for any hurt it may have caused."

Cincinnati Reds owner Marge Schott apologizing after the release of a deposition she gave a year earlier revealed her admission that she occasionally used the word "nigger" (though she wasn't sure that the word was offensive to blacks), that it was "possible" that she referred to Martin Luther King Jr.'s birthday as "Nigger Day," and that she possessed a swastika armband (though she had no idea why a Jewish employee of hers would be offended by that). *November 20, 1992*

—

"Wade Boggs is human and I'm sorry for what I did . . . I'm very sorry for what I did. I did not mean to ruin anyone's life when I started out doing this thing . . . You have to learn by the mistakes you make in life and go on and be a better person. Right now Wade Boggs is doing that and he is going to be a better person through all of this."

Boston Red Sox third baseman (and five-time American

League batting champion) Wade Boggs—married with two kids—apologizing in the semi-third person to his teammates and fans for the "unfortunate situation" created by the decision by his extracurricular paramour Margo Adams to go public in a *Penthouse* magazine article with various details about their four years together on Red Sox road trips. Among her revelations: Boggs's derisive comments about other Boston players (Jim Rice "thinks he's white," Roger Clemens was "Mr. Perfect" and Hall of Famer Ted Williams was "a guy that thinks he knows everything about hitting and doesn't"), details about the sex lives of Boggs and unnamed teammates involving threesomes and extramarital activities, and Boggs's superstitions ("One night I went to the game and he went 4-for-5. He found out that I hadn't worn panties underneath my dress. So for the next couple of months when he went into a slump, he'd ask me not to wear panties to the game ... It wasn't sexual, it was that he'd gotten hits and wanted to be sure of the little things he had done to get those hits"). Boggs chalked the whole thing up to his sex addiction, which he became aware of while "watching Geraldo Rivera a couple of weeks ago, and there was a show on about over-sexed people, and things like this, and Geraldo had psychologists on there and everything, and they were calling it a disease, and I feel that's exactly what happened—that a disease was taking over Wade Boggs, and it just did for four years." *February 1, 1989*

—

"I'm sincerely sorry. I made a stupid remark and I accept my punishment. I've apologized to Ms. Davis. There was no anti-Semitism whatsoever on my part."

Baseball umpire Bruce Froemming apologizing for referring to umpiring administrator Cathy Davis as a "stupid Jew bitch." *January 31, 2003*

⸻

"I made some mistakes and I think I'm being punished for those mistakes. However, the settlement is fair—especially the wording that says they have no finding that I bet on baseball. It's something I told the commissioner back in February and it's something I've told you people the last four months . . . My life is baseball. I hope to get back into baseball as soon as I possibly can. I'm looking forward to that. As a matter of fact, I've never looked forward to a birthday like I'm looking forward to my new daughter's birthday, 'cause two days after that is when I can apply for reinstatement."

Former Cincinnati Reds manager Pete Rose, disingenuously apologizing for his compulsive gambling as he embarked on a fifteen-year delusion that he could continue to deny betting on baseball and ever get reinstated. *August 24, 1989*

⸻

"I'm truly sorry about some of the statements I made yesterday. I realize it was something I should not have said even jokingly because of the seriousness of the situation. I grew up and have lived all my life in the Los Angeles area and would certainly not wish this destruction on anyone."

Dodgers outfielder Daryl Strawberry apologizing for saying about the wildfires blazing throughout Southern California, "Let it burn down, because I don't live there anymore." *November 3, 1993*

⸻

"I'm sorry for any ill will or any problem this has caused anyone else. I'm penitent, I'm contrite and I've been reprimanded. I put my foot in my mouth and I'm done with it."

University of Utah basketball coach Rick Majerus apologizing for telling a Milwaukee radio station, "You know, with women's athletics, my experience has been there's a great deal of, and I'll be frank with you here, there's a great deal of irregular sexual behavior." *October 16, 1989*

"I said a lot of things in the heat of the moment that I shouldn't have said. Called him names I shouldn't have called him. I apologize for that. I'm sorry. It was all meant to promote the fight."

Muhammad Ali apologizing for various insults—among them, "Uncle Tom" and "too ugly to be the champ"—he'd hurled at Joe Frazier back in the day. *March 15, 2001*

"I said I'm sorry. What else can I say? . . . I lied and I've admitted it. Life goes on."

Olympic sprinter Ben Johnson declaring that he's apologized enough to his fellow Canadians for having previously denied taking the steroids that were found in his system in 1988, disqualifying his hundred-meters victory at the summer games in Seoul. "Yes, I lied, but it's something I'm not ashamed of because everybody lied," he said. "Do you want me to drop down, kiss their feet, and say 'I'm sorry'?" *June 28, 1990*

"I sincerely regret and apologize for my remark last week concerning Mahmoud Abdul-Rauf and the national anthem. It was an offhand, off-the-cuff comment that was a very poor attempt at humor. It certainly does not reflect my true feelings. I respect Abdul-Rauf's right to express himself, and I feel badly about what I said."

Golfer Mike Sullivan apologizing for saying of Denver Nuggets guard Mahmoud Abdul-Rauf's refusal to stand when "The Star-Spangled Banner" was played, "I don't think they should suspend him. I think they should shoot him." *March 22, 1996*

———

"They can do whatever they want to do. This is the first time I've ever had a beef, and I've done maybe five hundred [dinner speeches] in my life. I apologize if I hurt anybody, but I don't know who I could have hurt. If they don't want to pay, there's nothing I can do about it. All I know is they had a sellout."

Jimmy "the Greek" Snyder apologizing for a speech delivered in Denver to a dinner audience of Colorado VIPs who paid five hundred dollars a plate to hear the authority on sports gambling deliver what one attendee described as "about three minutes of verbal abuse, insults and bigotry . . . There was a sense of sexism through the whole thing, racial references . . . then [a question-and-answer session] during which he insulted half the people by telling them their questions were stupid." Said another, "It wasn't a speech. It was just a very distasteful display of vulgarity by a person who seems to be a very crude individual." A third witness described Snyder's oration as "the most low-class speech we've ever had at any kind of benefit like that in Denver. It was profane, racially slanted—just a total embarrassment to everybody who was there." *June 6, 1984*

—

"Since the incident occurred, I haven't slept, nor have I been able to think clearly about anything else. I want everyone to know that I now realize that my actions on July twenty-fourth were very inappropriate."

New York Mets outfielder Vince Coleman apologizing to the parents of a two-year-old girl who sustained burns and other serious injuries from the explosion of a power-packed firecracker tossed out of a Jeep by Coleman in the Dodger Stadium parking lot. *July 29, 1993*

—

"First, I'd like to say Merry Christmas to all my friends, and I'd like to apologize to my neighborhood for all the disturbances I've caused. I'm feeling fine and I'm ready to start working out for the 1987 season. I'm looking forward to spending the holidays with my family here in Tampa. I still like Tampa and I'd like to continue to make it my home."

New York Mets pitcher Dwight Gooden apologizing for getting arrested after he and four friends got into a scuffle with police. *December 19, 1986*

—

"The statements I made about the NOW organization were careless and insensitive on my part. I had no right to make that statement about the NOW organization. It was wrong and I'm very sorry—and if I could take the comments back, I would."

Houston Astros pitcher Bob Knepper, who had recently said that "women were created in a role of submission to the husband," apologizing for telling *Sports Illustrated* that the National Organization for Women "is such a blowhard organization. They are a bunch of lesbians. Their focus has nothing to do with women's rights. It had everything to do with women wanting to be men." Knepper said at a press conference, "The comments I made were wrong because I know very little about the women in NOW. I feel that there's probably some very strong moral, upright women that believe very strongly in what they are doing in NOW." *June 18, 1988*

"I apologize for likening this situation to rape. It clearly is not a comparable situation and I was wrong to say that it was. I said something in an emotional moment that was insensitive and I am deeply sorry for it."

St. John's basketball coach Mike Jarvis apologizing for saying that the suspension of his star player Erick Barkley for an alleged NCAA rules violation felt like "someone had come into my house and raped me." *February 7, 2000*

"I would like to apologize to Jenny Worley, coach and athletic director Les Robinson and to East Tennessee State University for the incident following our contest. We in collegiate athletics must maintain a level of poise above reproach no matter how emotional and difficult the situation. We failed to do that . . . Please accept our sincere apologies."

University of Tennessee, Chattanooga basketball coach Mark McCarthy apologizing for his player Benny Green's reaction when a cheerleader from the victorious team stuck her finger in front of his face in a "We're Number One!" gesture—he smacked her in the face. *March 5, 1989*

—

"I do not think my action in the Purdue game was in any way necessary or appropriate. No one realizes that more than I do. I am certain that what I did in tossing the chair was an embarrassment to Indiana University. That was not my intention and for that reason I'm deeply sorry for it."

Indiana University basketball coach Bobby Knight apologizing for throwing a chair during a game in response to what he considered to be bad officiating. *February 24, 1985*

—

"This ain't no big controversy. I don't really even remember saying that. But when I say things after a game and I'm smiling about it, people should understand that it's a joke."

Philadelphia 76ers forward Charles Barkley apologizing for saying after a victory over the New Jersey Nets, "This is a game that if you lose, you go home and beat your wife and kids. Did you see my wife jumping up and down at the end of the game? That's because she knew I wasn't going to beat her." *November 24, 1990*

—

**"Dallas Green loves his wife, Sylvia, very much. They have a
wonderful family. She's his constant companion and he
regrets making his earlier statement and apologizes for
what has come from it."**

New York Mets PR director Jay Horwitz relaying manager
Dallas Green's apology for telling a reporter who wanted to
know how Green dealt with loss after loss, "I just beat the hell
out of Sylvia and kick the dog and whatever else I've got to do
to get it out." *August 4, 1993*

**"Despite the fact that I have been widely misquoted, there is
no doubt that I have been guilty of making some insensitive
remarks. And it is to the victims of my insensitivity that I
address these profound apologies."**

CBS golf announcer Ben Wright apologizing for telling the
Wilmington (DE) News-Journal that "lesbians in the sport
hurt women's golf" and that women golfers "are handicapped by having boobs"—quotes he'd spent half a year
denying. *January 9, 1996*

**"It was never my intention to hurt anyone. If my remarks
offended anyone, I am sorry."**

Chicago White Sox announcer Jimmy Piersall apologizing for calling baseball wives "horny broads." Said
Piersall, who was suspended for the last two weeks of the
season, "I didn't really think before I spoke." *September
18, 1981*

"I would like to start by once again publicly apologizing to Nancy Kerrigan. I realize, of course, that an apology coming from me rings hollow, but I was sorry after the act was committed and I'm sorry now."

Ice-skater Tonya Harding's ex-husband Jeff Gillooly apologizing in a Portland, OR, courtroom as he was sentenced to two years in jail for his role in organizing the kneecapping of his ex-wife's strongest Olympics rival. *July 13, 1994*

—

"Even though I was not involved in the procedure that took place, I take responsibility. If this incident was in any way not perceived as proper by those who love Mississippi State, then I apologize. If it caused any hardships to anyone here at the university, then I am sorry."

Mississippi State University football coach Jackie Sherrill apologizing for arranging—for "educational" and "motivational" purposes—the castration of a bull in front of his team during practice before a game against the University of Texas, whose team mascot was a steer. *September 15, 1992*

—

"I acknowledge that in the past I have, on occasion, made insensitive remarks which I now realize hurt others. On those few occasions, it was my mouth but not my heart speaking. I am profoundly sorry and I apologize to anyone I hurt. I can only say I did not mean them. I love baseball, and if anything I have said caused embarrassment to the game, the Reds, the wonderful fans and the city of Cincinnati, I am sorry . . . I know in my heart that I am not a racist or bigot."

Cincinnati Reds owner Marge Schott apologizing again in an

effort to stave off any repercussions from her past racist comments and actions. "As a minority person myself—a woman owner in the male baseball world—I have been on the receiving end of subtle and not-so-subtle discrimination," she pointed out. "Therefore, I am sensitive about comments which can hurt others." Two months later she was suspended from baseball for a year. *December 9, 1992*

———

"I would like to apologize for the incident that happened August twenty-sixth. I know I did a great injustice to St. Louis fans."

St. Louis Cardinals shortstop Garry Templeton apologizing for giving heckling fans the finger during a home game against the San Francisco Giants. A psychiatric evaluation showed him to be suffering from depression. *September 14, 1981*

———

"I feel they were wrong, and I feel I was wrong. I think I had my rights to do what I did, but I think I handled it the wrong way. I'd have showed I was a more mature person if I had ignored them and walked off the field."

Louisiana State University placekicker Ronnie Lewis apologizing "to the university, my teammates and my coaches" for giving booing fans the finger with both hands. *September 24, 1986*

———

"I want to apologize for my actions in the game against LSU. I realize there is no justifiable explanation for what I

did. I feel like I owe apologies to my family, friends, and teammates, and especially to the university which I represent."

University of Tennessee, Chattanooga, basketball center Doug Roth apologizing for giving heckling Louisiana State fans the finger. *February 13, 1989*

—

"What I did was totally unprofessional. I was wrong . . . I regret that I did it in front of kids. Kids are our future and they look up to guys like me."

Seattle SuperSonics center Benoit Benjamin apologizing for giving Los Angeles Clippers fans who booed him the finger. *April 9, 1991*

—

"I would like to apologize to all you fans, especially all of you young people out there. I was wrong in what I did. I'm an intense player and I lost control of my emotions. I was wrong and I apologize for it."

University of Hawaii forward John Molle Jr. apologizing for twice giving hostile fans the finger during the Western Athletic Conference tournament. *March 11, 1995*

—

"I still consider myself to be a positive role model, and I hope that my actions have not changed the public's perception of me. I am truly sorry, and I will try my best not to let it happen [again]."

Washington Bullets forward Juwan Howard apologizing for his behavior after fouling out of a game, which consisted of knocking over a microphone, kicking over a watercooler, and, after being ejected for those actions, giving the finger as he departed. *February 28, 1996*

—

"I want to offer my apologies to Rocky Marciano's family for remarks I made at the press conference. If I hurt Marciano's family, I regret it."

Former heavyweight champion Larry Holmes apologizing for telling Marciano's brother Peter, after failing to tie Marciano's 49–0 record by losing his bout with Michael Spinks, "Rocky couldn't carry my jockstrap." *September 23, 1985*

—

"Well, the only thing I'd like to say is it's an embarrassment to me and the Minnesota Vikings and an apology is on order."

Wide receiver Hassan Jones apologizing for being the sixth member of his team in the last year to be arrested for drunk driving. *November 16, 1987*

—

"During the course of that program, I made some statements regarding what I perceive to be the reasons why there are no black managers or general managers in major league baseball today. My statements have been misconstrued as indicating a belief that blacks lack the ability to hold such positions. I hold no such beliefs. However, I and only I am responsible for my statements. Therefore I apologize to the American people and particularly to all black Americans for

my statement and for my inability under the circumstances to express accurately my beliefs . . . In my work and in my personal life I have never distinguished a person by reason of his color, but only by reason of his ability. For this reason, I feel that this is the saddest moment in my entire career."

Los Angeles Dodgers vice president Al Campanis apologizing for his disastrous *Nightline* appearance (on a show celebrating the fortieth anniversary of Jackie Robinson's becoming the first black player in the major leagues) in which he said of black athletes, "I truly believe they may not have some of the necessities to be, let's say, a field manager or perhaps a general manager. So it just might be—why are black men, or black people, not good swimmers? They just don't have the buoyancy. I don't say all of them, but how many quarterbacks do you have, how many pitchers do you have, that are black? . . . You have to pay your dues to become a manager. Generally, you have to go to the minor leagues. There's not much pay involved and some of the better-known black players have been able to get into better fields, and make a better living in that way." Though team officials insisted his job was not in jeopardy, he was fired the day after his apology after forty-three years with the team. *April 7, 1987*

"If what I said offended people, I apologize. I didn't mean for my remarks to come out the way they did. I was trying to emphasize how much harder so many blacks work at becoming better athletes than white athletes. And they work harder because they're hungrier. That many black athletes run faster and jump higher than whites is a fact. Using the term 'bred' was wrong on my part and I apologize for that,

as I do for suggesting coaching was the only domain left for whites. Blacks could do well in that area, too, if given the opportunity."

CBS Sports commentator Jimmy "the Greek" Snyder apologizing for an interview he gave to a Washington, D.C., TV station that was using Martin Luther King Jr.'s birthday as a jumping-off point for a look at how much progress blacks had made in American society. Among Snyder's observations: he said blacks had been "bred to be the better athlete," a tradition dating back to pre–Civil War days when "the slave owner would breed his big black with his big woman so that he would have a big black kid. That's where it all started." He warned, "If they take over coaching jobs like everybody wants them to, there's not going to be anything left for the white people." And why did he think blacks were better athletes? "Now that's because they practice and they play and practice and play. They're not lazy like the white athlete is." So, overall, his assessment of the interview? "I should have expressed myself a lot better than I did today." *January 15, 1988*

—

"I feel quite poorly. What else could I say about it? Of course, I apologize to everybody. Please let me alone for the rest of the day. I got enough headaches right now. I mean, I'm seventy years old and I've never been in trouble in my life over anything like this. I didn't think I said anything. Please, please, I don't want to make it any worse for CBS than it already is."

Jimmy "the Greek" Snyder continuing to apologize. *January 16, 1988*

—

"It would do no good to explain that I was actually trying to say something very positive about black athletes—that they work hard, they are disciplined, they overcome great obstacles and odds to become great athletes and they are highly motivated . . . Thus, the only thing I know to do as a human being is to say I'm sorry, offer my regrets and ask for forgiveness. In all honesty, more than the loss of my job at CBS, the thing that hurts me most is the loss of your respect for me. The job I can do without. I need my self-respect back. The only way I know how to do that is to ask for forgiveness from the people I have offended—Americans generally, black Americans in particular, and black athletes especially. That's why I'm writing you—to ask for your forgiveness."

> Jimmy "the Greek" Snyder, fired by CBS after a twelve-year association, apologizing in a letter to civil rights groups and players' associations. *January 17, 1988*

"I am truly sorry for what has happened, and not just because I have had to leave baseball, the sport I love, and face still more punishment because of my mistakes. My family and friends have suffered as well, and I regret the pain I have caused them. I mean that from the bottom of my heart. I also realize that millions of baseball fans may have been disappointed because I didn't live up to the respect and admiration they gave me during my career. I am not a bad person, but I did some bad things."

> Pete Rose apologizing for the gambling problems—at least the ones he was willing to admit to—for which he was suspended from baseball while pleading guilty to two felony tax charges. *April 20, 1990*

—

"Saturday night was the worst night of my professional career as a boxer and I am here today to apologize, to ask the people who expected more from Mike Tyson to forgive me for snapping in that ring and doing something that I have never done before and will never do again. I apologize to the world . . . I just snapped . . . For an athlete in the heat of battle to suddenly lose it is not new but it's not right and for me it doesn't change anything. I was wrong . . . Now I will continue to train not just my body but my mind too, so that if it's possible I can put this behind me and so that I will know that it can never happen again. I only ask that you forgive me as you have forgiven others of us in professional sports so that I can be given a chance to redeem myself when my family, my friends, my doctors, and most of all, my God tell me I am ready to do so. Thank you."

Mike Tyson apologizing for biting off a chunk of heavyweight champion Evander Holyfield's right ear during the third round of their Las Vegas title bout, and then getting himself disqualified by biting Holyfield's left ear. *June 30, 1997*

—

"My comments were not intended to be racially derogatory. Everyone who knows me knows that I'm a jokester, but that is no excuse for what I said. Jokes aren't funny when they hurt people. I realize that what I said has hurt many people and I apologize to anyone who was offended."

Golfer Fuzzy Zoeller apologizing for referring to the first black (well, actually one-fourth black) Masters winner Tiger Woods as "that little boy" and urging him (as the champion who will pick the menu for the next Champions Dinner) "not

to serve fried chicken next year . . . Or collard greens or whatever the hell they serve." *April 21, 1997*

⸺

**"It's very important to me that people understand that I
didn't mean for the situation to turn out like it did . . . I also
regret and apologize to fans who were upset by what
happened . . . I have total respect for all the players who play
the game, and I respect [NBA Commissioner] David Stern
but I don't think he has been fair with me in this situation."**

Frequently suspended and fined Indiana Pacers forward Ron
Artest (who had recently asked for time off from the NBA season
to promote an R&B CD on his new record label) apologizing for
igniting a mêlée between players and fans by charging into the
Detroit stands during a game against the Pistons and viciously
punching a fan who he believed threw a cup at him, while at the
same time complaining that his seventy-three-game suspension
without pay, which would cost him over five million dollars, was
too severe a punishment. *November 21, 2004*

⸺

**"I'd like to apologize for what I've done. I've let a lot of
people down. For the first time, I'm beginning to understand my problem."**

San Diego Padres pitcher LaMarr Hoyt apologizing for trying
to walk across the San Ysidro border from Mexico carrying
more than three hundred Valiums, 138 propoxyphenes, and
three joints. As this was his third drug arrest in nine
months—and his second at this border crossing—he was
sentenced to forty-five days in jail. *December 16, 1986*

⸺

"I deeply regret my disrespectful conduct towards a man that I know always gives his utmost as an umpire. I'm sincerely sorry that my actions deeply offended John and, by engaging in indefensible conduct, I failed the game of baseball, the Orioles organization and my fellow major leaguers."

Baltimore Orioles second baseman Roberto Alomar apologizing for spitting in umpire John Hirschbeck's face (for which he received a five-game suspension) and telling reporters afterward that he "used to respect" the umpire but after the man's eight-year-old son died, "he just changed, personality-wise. He just got real bitter." Alomar's apology was accompanied by the pledge of a $50,000 contribution to help fight the brain disease that claimed Hirschbeck's son. *September 30, 1996*

"On Wednesday night, I made an off-the-cuff insensitive comment that could be misconstrued as offensive. Friends, please accept my profound apologies. They're from the bottom of my heart."

Miami Heat announcer David Halberstam apologizing for saying, "When Thomas Jefferson was around, basketball was not invented yet, but those slaves working at Thomas Jefferson's farm, I'm sure they would have made good basketball players." *March 21, 1997*

"I've known Ms. Perhach for ten years. We've had this relationship. As I said a moment ago, I'm sorry if she felt she was harmed."

NBC (and NBA and NHL) sportscaster Marv Albert apologizing in court to Vanessa Perhach, whose accusations of sexual assault against him (she was treated for more than a dozen back bites) led to two days of lurid testimony about his sex life (Marv in women's panties? Allegedly, *yessss!*) that he was only able to end by plea-bargaining. "In the past, there was consensual biting," Albert testified. "On this particular evening, I did not realize until her testimony that she felt she was harmed. For that I am sorry." Though he received no jail time, he did pay the public man's price of being off the air for a while, but then he was allowed back. *October 24, 1997*

———

"I am sorry if I offended anyone with a remark I made during a speech on Wednesday. I did not mean to say anything insensitive. What I was trying to say was that I am quite proud that our players have traditionally been clean-shaven and earring-free while wearing a Cincinnati Reds uniform. I am a staunch defender of the tradition of baseball. We try to set a good example for the young baseball fans at Riverfront Stadium and across the country."

Cincinnati Reds owner Marge Schott, back in baseball after a one-year suspension for racial and ethnic slurs, apologizing for saying that "only fruits wear earrings." *May 20, 1994*

———

"I regret that I lost my spirituality for an instance. It will not happen again."

Cleveland Indians outfielder Albert Belle apologizing after receiving a seven-day suspension for throwing a ball into the

chest of a fan who teased him about his drinking problems
and invited him to a "keg party." *May 13, 1991*

———

"You're a blessing. You're a piece of my heart. You're the air
I breathe. You're the strongest person I know. I'm so sorry I
put you through this, that I put our family through this."

Los Angeles Lakers guard Kobe Bryant at a nationally tele-
vised Staples Center news conference, apologizing to his
wife, Vanessa, for having sex at a Colorado resort with a nine-
teen-year-old woman who went on to charge him with rape.
July 18, 2003

———

"First, I want to apologize directly to the young woman
involved in this incident. I want to apologize to her for my
behavior that night and for the consequences she has suffered
in the past year . . . Although I truly believe this encounter
between us was consensual, I recognize now that she did not
and does not view this incident the same way I did. After
months of reviewing discovery, listening to her attorney, and
even her testimony in person, I now understand how she feels
that she did not consent to this encounter."

Los Angeles Lakers guard Kobe Bryant apologizing to the
woman who accused him of raping her after the charge
against him was dropped due to her unwillingness to pursue
the case any further. *September 1, 2004*

———

"I want everyone to know how sorry I am for what happened
. . . I'm not as bad as everyone has made me out to be. It's

as if I'm another O. J. Simpson. Yes, I was wrong, but I didn't kill anybody. I'm not a double murderer. No matter what happens, I hope to sit down with P. J. some day and have a long conversation. I want to look in his eyes so he can see how sincere I am in my apology. I wish I had taken the time to sit down before."

Former Golden State Warriors guard Latrell Sprewell apologizing for choking coach P. J. Carlesimo during a team practice. *January 23, 1998*

—

"I apologize to anyone who is sensitive to what I said, but I'm not apologizing for people thinking I'm a racist."

CBS college basketball analyst Billy Packer apologizing for referring to black Georgetown University guard Allen Iverson as "a tough monkey," which he said "had absolutely nothing to do with anything to do with race." Explained Packer, "I have great respect for the way he plays. He's fearless. He's become a total basketball player in every way. So maybe that's no political correctness, but I have great admiration for that kid." *March 5, 1996*

—

"There are few words to describe how awful I feel and what I have experienced within these last twenty-four hours. I've been a Cub fan all my life and fully understand the relationship between my actions and the outcome of the game. I had my eyes glued on the approaching ball the entire time and was so caught up in the moment that I did not even see Moises Alou, much less that he may have had a play. Had I thought for one second that the ball was playable or had I

seen Alou approaching I would have done whatever I could
to get out of the way and give Alou a chance to make the
catch. To Moises Alou, the Chicago Cubs organization, Ron
Santo, Ernie Banks, and Cub fans everywhere I am so truly
sorry from the bottom of this Cubs fan's broken heart."

Mortified Cubs fan Steve Bartman apologizing for his inter-
ference with a foul ball, which allowed the batter to walk
instead of fouling out, which allowed the Florida Marlins—
behind 3–0 in the eighth inning of the sixth game of the play-
offs—to score eight runs and win the game, which forced a
seventh game that the Cubs, of course, lost. *October 15, 2003*

"I feel I owe an apology to Bulls fans for my conduct during
the game last night and my comments following the game."

Chicago Bulls forward Scottie Pippin apologizing for giving
booing fans the finger ("I thought about it last night when I was
home and throughout the night. It was something I thought
about and I knew I had to deal with . . . I'm sorry I made the
gesture") and for saying he'd "never seen a white guy get
booed" at Chicago Stadium ("In past years, they have booed
players of both races"). *March 1, 1994*

"I want to apologize for the incident that happened in
Miami. It's an embarrassment to me, but also for the Green
Bay Packer organization."

Najeh Davenport, a University of Miami fullback newly
drafted by the Packers, apologizing for his arrest for breaking
into a coed's dorm and defecating in her closet. *July 25, 2002*

"Those people that know me know that I have a sense of humor. I would never seriously say something derogatory to people. If I offended anyone, I'm sorry . . . I apologize that some people don't have a sense of humor like I do. Because when I did it, the whole room laughed. It's nothing personal. But to say I'm racist against Asians is crazy . . . I'm an idiot prankster . . . At times I try to be a comedian. Sometimes I say good jokes, sometimes I say bad jokes. If I hurt anybody's feelings, I apologize."

Los Angeles Lakers center Shaquille O'Neal apologizing for a moment six months earlier—which the media had only just caught up with—when he looked into a TV camera and taunted his Houston Rockets counterpart by saying, "Tell Yao Ming, 'Ching-chong-yang-wah-ah-soh.'" *January 10, 2003*

—

"I love Irina Spirlea. I don't see any prejudice at all. I met with her and apologized for making a stupid statement. She's a professional, and I shouldn't have talked about her that way."

Richard Williams, father of tennis pros Venus and Serena, apologizing for accusing Irina Spirlea of racism—and calling her "a big, tall, white turkey"—after she bumped into Venus during a U.S. Open changeover. *January 22, 1998*

—

"To every single Philadelphia Eagles fan out there that cheers for me, I want you to know that I'm sorry this has happened. To you I apologize . . . Also, I would like to re-iterate my respect for Donovan McNabb, as a quarterback and as a teammate. I apologize to him for any comments that may have been negative . . . To my head coach, Andy

Reid, I owe you an apology . . . To [Eagles president] Joe Banner and [Eagles owner] Mr. Lurie, I understand that all along you were trying to do what you believed in the best interests for the team, the Philadelphia Eagles. I apologize to both of you."

Philadelphia Eagles wide receiver Terrell Owens multi-apologizing for having given an interview to ESPN.com in which he complained about his quarterback and self-pityingly said of his team's failure to stop the October 23 game against the San Diego Chargers to make a big fuss over his hundredth touchdown catch, "It's an embarrassment. It just shows a lack of class they have . . . Had it been somebody else, they probably would have popped fireworks around the stadium." *November 8, 2005*

====

"It was just a flippant remark that was addressed to the question and then I said, 'Just kidding.' Everybody heard it was a joke . . . It was not a thought-out question and not a thought-out response to the question. It was a joking response to the question with no malicious intent at all. If I have offended anyone by that, I wholeheartedly apologize."

Earl Woods, author of *Training a Tiger: A Father's Guide to Raising a Winner in Both Golf and Life*, apologizing for his appearance with his son at a Kennedy Center speaking engagement where he answered the question, "What book, other than your own . . . has most inspired you?" with the unexpected response, "*Mein Kampf.*" *November 10, 1998*

====

"I'm sure that I'm supposed to act all sorry or sad or guilty now that I've accepted that I've done something wrong. But you see, I'm just not built that way. Sure, there's probably some real emotion buried somewhere deep inside. And maybe I'd be a better person if I let that side of my personality come out. But it just doesn't surface too often. So let's leave it like this . . . I'm sorry it happened, and I'm sorry for all the people, fans and family that it hurt. Let's move on."

Pete Rose, who ended his decade-and-a-half denial that he ever bet on baseball with an admission in his second autobiography, *Pete Rose: My Prison Without Bars*, apologizing in the epilogue. *January 6, 2004*

—

"I totally regret the situation. Naturally, it's very embarrassing. Not only to myself, but to my family and the New York Yankees. It's an unfortunate situation that escalated a little bit."

Yankees third baseman Wade Boggs apologizing for causing Continental flight attendant Karen Plympton to file a verbal harassment lawsuit against him by saying, among many other unpleasant things, that he would "kick her fat lips in" for not bringing him a final beer as the plane was preparing to land. *August 1, 1996*

—

"I am very sorry that my remarks on ESPN last Sunday offended many people. This was not my intent at all. Sometimes I do not always express myself well, as in this instance. Let me take this opportunity to set the record straight. I do not and have never condoned Adolf Hitler's policies of hatred, militarism and genocide. Hitler was unquestionably one of history's most despicable tyrants. Anyone who knows me knows how much I respect the brave soldiers who sacrificed so much to defeat the Nazis in World War II. I also know that many American families, including mine, had relatives in Europe who suffered greatly during the war. It is distressing that my comments did not adequately convey my true feelings. I will continue to try to be more sensitive to all people, and in the future will be more careful of what I say and to whom. The last thing I wish to do is offend anyone, or embarrass the Reds, the city of Cincinnati or the great American game of baseball."

Cincinnati Reds owner Marge Schott apologizing for a pro-Hitler comment: "Everything you read, when he came in he was good. They built tremendous highways and got all the factories going. He went nuts, he went berserk. I think his own generals tried to kill him, didn't they? Everybody knows he was good at the beginning, but he just went too far." *May 7, 1996*

—

"While I have evidenced strong competitive feelings about New York fans in the past and take responsibility for things I have said publicly, including the *Sports Illustrated* article, I recognize that I have gone way too far in my competitive zeal. I want everybody to understand that my emotions fuel my competitive zeal. They are a source of energy for me; however, I have let my emotions get the best of my judgment and have said things which, read with cold, hard logic, are unacceptable to me and to my country. Even though it might appear otherwise from what I've said, I am not a racist. I should not have said what I did because it is not what I believe in my heart . . . Everyone makes mistakes . . . I am contrite."

Atlanta Braves relief pitcher and Georgia native John Rocker apologizing by blaming his "competitive zeal" for a breathtaking display of bigotry the likes of which most humans never come close to allowing themselves to reveal. Having established his loathing for Mets fans by spitting at them and giving them frequent fingers, Rocker unleashed his contempt for their city in a *Sports Illustrated* interview in which he shared some of his pet peeves, among them immigrants ("I'm not a very big fan of foreigners. You can walk an entire block in Times Square and not hear anybody speaking English. Asians and Koreans and Vietnamese and Indians and Russians and Spanish people and everything up there. How the hell did they get in this country?") and the kind of lowlifes one finds on the subway ("some kid with purple hair next to some queer with AIDS right next to some dude who just got out of jail for the fourth time right next to some twenty-year-old mom with four kids"). The hue and cry was deafening, suspensions and fines were levied, and though he claimed to "fully intend to learn from this experience," in fact he remained every inch the lout, making news a few months later with an angry threat to the *Sports Illustrated* reporter ("Do you know what I could do to you?" he screamed) and a few years later when he called a gay male couple "fruitcakes" ("I admit I was angry and said some things I probably should not have said," he apologized then, "but I wanted to make it clear their attentions were unwelcome"). The day after the self-immolating interview appeared, Braves pitching coach

Leo Mazzone was strikingly prescient. "Baseball's a very humbling game," he said. "Something's going to go wrong now with his career. And you watch it, it'll end up going straight down the tubes." And that's just what happened. *December 22, 1999*

The Disarmed Forces

"We apologize to the women involved, the Navy and the nation for our part in what has become a source of embarrassment . . . In hindsight, we recognize the errors that contributed to the possibility of partygoers getting out of hand. We will correct those errors in the future. We've had our wake-up call."

The Tailhook Association apologizing for the sexual abuse suffered by upward of twenty-five women at the aviator group's 1991 convention in Las Vegas who said they'd been groped, fondled, and sexually assaulted by drunken Navy fliers. One change planned for future conventions, according to Tailhook spokesperson Steve Millikin: there will be "control over the use of alcohol." *August 7, 1992*

—

"I am not anti-Islam or any other religion. I support the free exercise of all religions. For those who have been offended by my statements, I offer a sincere apology."

Army Lt. Gen. William G. Boykin apologizing for repeatedly describing the war on terrorism as a battle between a "Christian army" and Satan, and for saying of a captured Somali warlord who'd said he'd be protected by Allah, "I knew that my God was bigger than his. I knew that my God was a real God, and his was an idol." *October 17, 2003*

━━

"I apologize to the Marine Corps and all current and former Marines for my remarks. My point—ineptly put—was that all the services had different relationships with civilian society, based in part on their culture, the size of their force and their mission."

Sara Lister, the Army's top personnel official, apologizing for telling a public seminar that her branch of the armed services was "much more connected to society than the Marines are. The Marines are extremists. Wherever you have extremists, you've got some risks of total disconnection with society. And that's a little dangerous." *November 13, 1997*

━━

"All fault is mine. I can't ask for forgiveness. This is a burden I will carry to the grave."

Cdr. Scott Waddle apologizing at a Tokyo court of inquiry to the families of nine people killed when the surfacing submarine USS *Greeneville* sank a Japanese high school's training ship. Further complicating this international incident were reports that two civilians were at the sub's controls at the time, though the Navy insisted that they were "under the direct supervision" of crew members. *February 28, 2001*

━━

"I regret it now as a tasteless prank, and I'm sorry I did it."

Army Spc. 4 Michael Franklin apologizing for perpetrating a hoax on ten-year-old Heather McGinn by sending her a letter claiming that a pink balloon she released in Monroeville, PA, as part of a national *Weekly Reader*–sponsored contest to see whose balloon would travel the farthest had made it—after an eight-week trip—to the West German–East German border. Though the deadline for winning the contest had passed, Heather became a local celebrity, only to find out that Franklin had actually found the balloon, many weeks earlier, a mere 150 miles from its launch site, and brought it with him when he was shipped overseas to Heidelberg. "I think she'll be a little disillusioned about believing people," her mother said. "It was an exciting thing for her to think her balloon had traveled that far. And of course, children are very trusting." *May 24, 1985*

"Hundreds of thousands of military draftees served over the years with great distinction and valor—many being wounded and still others killed. The last thing I would want to do would be to disparage the service of those draftees . . . I always have had the highest respect for their service, and I offer my full apology to any veteran who misinterpreted my remarks when I said them."

Defense Secretary Donald Rumsfeld apologizing for his "not eloquently stated" observation opposing reinstatement of the draft because inductees served for relatively short periods of time after many costly months of training, "adding no value, no advantage" to the military. *January 21, 2003*

"We are deeply sorry for what has happened to these people and what the families must be feeling. It's just not right. And we will get to the bottom of what happened. It's simply unacceptable that anyone would engage in the abuse of Iraqi prisoners."

National security adviser Condoleezza Rice apologizing for

the abuse, humiliation, and torture inflicted on Iraqis at Abu Ghraib prison. *May 4, 2004*

——

"My Army has been embarrassed by this. My Army has been shamed by this. And on behalf of my Army, I apologize for what those soldiers did to your citizens. It was reprehensible and it was unacceptable."

Brig. Gen. Mark Kimmitt, spokesman for the U.S. command in Iraq. *May 5, 2004*

——

"To those Iraqis who were mistreated by members of the U.S. armed forces, I offer my deepest apology. It was inconsistent with the values of our nation, it was inconsistent with the teachings of the military to the men and women of the armed forces, and it was certainly fundamentally un-American."

Defense Secretary Donald Rumsfeld. *May 7, 2004*

——

"As a soldier and military police officer, I failed my duties and failed my mission to protect and defend. I not only let down the people in Iraq, but I let down every single soldier that serves today. My actions potentially caused an increased hatred and insurgency towards the United States, putting soldiers and civilians at greater risk. I take full responsibility for my actions . . . The decisions I made were mine and mine alone."

Spc. Sabrina Harman apologizing for abusing Iraqi detainees at Abu Ghraib prison. *May 17, 2005*

—

"I know this has caused you great concern and I sincerely apologize for the error. I am pleased to now set the record straight."

Brig. Gen. John M. Gosdin apologizing to Army Reserve Spc. Jacqueline Ortiz for the Army's earlier response to her accusation of sexual assault against 1st Sgt. David Martinez, which was not to prosecute him for forcing her to perform oral sex but, rather, to place a letter of reprimand in her file for fraternizing with a higher-ranked officer. *May 22, 1992*

—

"I made a serious mistake this morning. My recent comment was the result of my frustration over the stupidity of this heinous and incomprehensible crime against the young lady. I regret any misunderstanding my comment may have caused."

Adm. Richard C. Macke, commander of U.S. forces in the Pacific, apologizing for having observed that the three American servicemen who raped a twelve-year-old Okinawan girl would have been better off if they'd taken the money they spent to rent a car and rented a prostitute instead—a comment that led to his forced early retirement. *November 17, 1995*

—

"I wish to make it perfectly clear that I have the greatest admiration and respect for the governor, the vice governors, Mayor Yoshida and the members of the Diet. If my remarks in the e-mail are construed as suggesting anything else, then I am deeply sorry and apologize for the misunderstanding."

Lt. Gen. Earl Hailston, chief of U.S. military forces on the Japanese island of Okinawa, apologizing for an e-mail— apparently prompted by the arrest of a U.S. Marine for lifting a local high school girl's skirt and taking photos—in which he said of Okinawan officials, "I think they are all nuts and a bunch of wimps." *February 6, 2001*

"I apologize to the American public for that. I am very sorry for it. It was a failure of the standards that should be put to public officials like myself."

Former Pentagon official Daniel Ellsberg apologizing for not having gone public in 1964, when it could have made a difference, with the documents in his possession showing Lyndon Johnson's plans to escalate the Vietnam War. *April 8, 1997*

"Just let me say to each of you who have worked so hard and taken such risks to cover this story, I extend a heartfelt apology and hope you will accept it. I understand well the enormous dangers that you face, and want to restate my admiration for your professionalism, dedication, and, yes, courage."

Deputy Defense Secretary Paul Wolfowitz apologizing for saying that media coverage of the Iraq war failed to accentuate the positive because "a lot of the press are afraid to travel very much, so they sit in Baghdad and they publish rumors. And rumors are plentiful." *June 24, 2004*

"Oh, Lord! I'm just sorry. I'm just so sorry for what I did."

Army Staff Sgt. Vernell Robinson Jr. apologizing for having

sex—often not the consensual kind—with five female trainees. "I got the devil in me," he said at his sentencing hearing, repeatedly bashing his head on the witness stand. "I don't know what happened. I don't know what happened. This thing is so bad." *May 30, 1997*

Facing the Music

"To whatever extent somebody was wounded, I am very sorry. That was never my intention."

Singer Pat Boone apologizing for appearing at the American Music Awards in a studded dog collar, sporting fake tattoos, and with his chest bare beneath a leather outfit to promote his new album *In a Metal Mood: No More Mr. Nice Guy.* "I was really stunned that Christians, evidently by the thousands, having known me for thirty-five to forty years, would think that overnight I just radically changed my orientation and all my priorities," Boone said. "If we have to apologize for making a joke, then we're in big trouble." *April 15, 1997*

"I think I handled it badly because I got uptight. I wanted it to be perfect and I'm not perfect. I'm normal."

Singer Diana Ross apologizing for screaming at her sound crew and kicking a monitor off of its platform during her opening night concert at London's Wembley Arena. *June 4, 1982*

"It was never our intention to offend anyone or upset the family of the late Elvis Presley."

The Memphis Jaycees apologizing to the Elvis Presley estate for a charity-raising haunted house that featured a "Dead Elvis" exhibit: an Elvis impersonator in a coffin, empty pizza boxes, partly eaten jelly doughnuts, pill bottles, and a toilet, the latter two of which were removed in response to protests. *October 28, 1991*

—

"We're very sorry to have made them unhappy. We ourselves have not been happy that we were not allowed to sing on our albums. We're relieved that the truth has now been made public."

Rob Pilatus of Milli Vanilli apologizing to fans after the pop duo was stripped of its Best New Artist Grammy when it was revealed that neither he nor partner Fabrice Morvan sang a note on their debut album, *Girl You Know It's True*. *November 20, 1990*

—

"There has been a lot of controversy about my song 'They Don't Care About Us.' My intention was for this song to say 'no' to racism, anti-Semitism and stereotyping. Unfortunately my choice of words may have unintentionally hurt the very people I wanted to stand in solidarity with. I just want you all to know how strongly I am committed to tolerance, peace and love, and I apologize to anyone who might have been hurt."

Michael Jackson, who claimed to have been "truly surprised, shocked and deeply hurt at the unforeseen reaction that the lyrics of 'They Don't Care About Us' have caused," apologizing for the lines "Jew me, sue me, everybody do me / Kick me, kike me, don't you black or white me." Said Rabbi Abraham Cooper of L.A.'s Simon Wiesenthal Center, "Mr. Jackson assured me on the phone that he didn't have a single racist bone in his body. But he now understands that lyrics that included the word 'kike' could easily be misconstrued by his fans." And Jackson told Diane Sawyer on *Primetime Live* that some of his best friends—actually, his "three best friends . . . David Geffen, Jeffrey Katzenberg, [and] Steven Spielberg"—are Jewish. *June 16, 1995*

⸻

"The tearing of Janet Jackson's costume was unrehearsed, unplanned, completely unintentional and was inconsistent with assurances we had about the content of the performance. MTV regrets this incident occurred and we apologize to anyone who was offended by it."

MTV apologizing for the brief exposure of Janet Jackson's right breast during the halftime show at Super Bowl XXXVIII. Still, one had to wonder what the choreographer who promised "shocking moments" had in mind if not this. *February 1, 2004*

⸻

"I am sorry that anyone was offended by the wardrobe malfunction during the halftime performance of the Super Bowl. It was not intentional and is regrettable."

Justin Timberlake, who pulled off the leather cup covering Jackson's breast at the end of their duet, as they sang, "Gonna have you naked by the end of this song." *February 1, 2004*

⸻

"The decision to have a costume reveal at the end of my half-time show performance was made after final rehearsals. MTV was completely unaware of it. It was not my intention that it go as far as it did. I apologize to anyone offended—including the audience, MTV, CBS and the NFL."

> Janet Jackson, ignorant of the cultural witch hunt her little publicity stunt just provided the excuse for. *February 2, 2004*

—

"It upsets me to think that 'Black or White' could influence any child or adult to destructive behavior, either sexual or violent. I've always tried to be a good role model and therefore have made these changes to avoid any possibility of adversely affecting any individual's behavior. I deeply regret any pain or hurt that the final segment of 'Black or White' has caused children, their parents or any other viewers."

> Michael Jackson apologizing for a four-minute epilogue to his new video (promoting his new album *Dangerous*) in which he smashes a car with a crowbar, unzips his fly, and simulates masturbation. *November 15, 1991*

—

"I want to apologize for the things I used to say and show to you. The other day, I heard that stupid song I used to sing, 'Nasty Girls.' You don't listen to stuff like that, right?"

> Denise Smith apologizing from the pulpit of a Riverdale, MD, church for her former life as the Prince protégé Vanity. *June 1, 1997*

—

"If I offended some people, I am sorry. I did not mean to offend them by distributing the words of God."

Singer Yoko Ono apologizing for ripping pages out of a Bible during her concert at New York's Irving Plaza and tossing them to fans while quoting the Beatles song "Julia": "Half of what I say is meaningless, but I say it just to reach you." *May 16, 1996*

—

"We regret that last night's telecast . . . contained some offensive language. This has not happened before in the seventeen years that the awards show has been on the air and we will take precautionary measures to see that it will not happen in future telecasts."

ABC spokesperson Janice Gretemeyer apologizing for profanities uttered by Guns N' Roses guitarists Duff McKagan and Slash while accepting their American Music Awards for favorite heavy metal group and best heavy metal album. *January 22, 1990*

—

"The truth is I messed up. I understand the anger of the fans, who spent their time and money to come to the show. And the best I can do at this point is to refund their money and say I'm sorry."

Country singer Hank Williams Jr. apologizing for ending a Kansas City, KS, concert after only fifteen minutes when fans reacted badly to the drunkenness that prevented him from enunciating—or even remembering—his lyrics. "He could barely walk," said Jim Beard of the Wyandotte County Sheriff's Department. "He wasn't even playing his guitar. He was just holding it." *July 29, 1992*

—

"We don't stand for hatred. We're not here to make enemies. We're apologizing to anyone who might be offended by Griff's remarks."

Rapper Chuck D., leader of Public Enemy, apologizing for a statement by newly fired group member Richard "Professor Griff" Griffin in which he said that Jews caused "the majority of wickedness that goes on across the globe" (with a particular focus on the treatment of blacks in South Africa), raised the question, "Is it a coincidence that the Jews run the jewelry business and it's named Jewelry?" and answered that question: "No coincidence." *June 21, 1989*

—

"As a concerned American citizen, I apologize to President Bush because my remark was disrespectful. I feel that whoever holds that office should be treated with the utmost respect."

Natalie Maines of the Texas-based Dixie Chicks apologizing for telling a London audience, "Just so you know, we're ashamed the president of the United States is from Texas." The apology seemed less heartfelt than her defense of the offending remark a day earlier: "I feel the president is ignoring the opinion of many in the U.S. and alienating the rest of the world. My comments were made in frustration, and one of the privileges of being an American is you are free to voice your own point of view." *March 14, 2003*

—

"If anything I have said has hurt Billy Ray Cyrus or his family, I apologize. But I don't apologize for my opinion."

Country singer Travis Tritt apologizing for offering this critique: "I'll be honest. I don't think 'Achy Breaky Heart' makes much of a statement. I just don't care much for the song. I didn't care for the way the video was presented, as if he were drawing 15,000 people into a concert hall. He's stepping out of a limousine and being mobbed as he goes into a concert. This is a guy that's not even been recognized yet. This is his first single." *June 13, 1992*

—

"I just want to set the record straight. In 1986, I harassed a group of schoolkids on a field trip. Many of the students were African Americans. In 1988, I assaulted two Vietnamese men over a case of beer. Racist slurs and language were used during these encounters, and people were seriously hurt. I am truly sorry for what I did. I was a teenager and intoxicated when I did these things, but that's no excuse. Nor is it okay to beat up people because your friends are doing it. I know there are kids out there doing the same stuff now, and I just want to tell them, 'Don't do it.' Asian Pacific Americans, African Americans, and all people have the right to live free of violence and harassment. I want to make it clear that I condemn antigay hatred and violence."

White rapper Marky Mark apologizing in a statement read by his manager while standing underneath an enormous Times Square billboard featuring Mark in his Calvin Klein underwear. *February 18, 1993*

—

"I clearly got carried away in the theatrics of the moment and I now realize how inappropriate and wrong my actions were."

Red Hot Chili Peppers drummer Chad Smith apologizing for sexually harassing a college coed at a Daytona Beach taping of an MTV *Spring Break* show by spanking her and attempting to remove her swimsuit bottom while fellow band member Michael "Flea" Balzary knelt on her legs and demanded that she fellate him. *August 9, 1990*

—

"If anyone feels hurt by what I said at the press conference, I ask their forgiveness, because I have never felt or thought what was read into my words."

German composer Karlheinz Stockhausen apologizing for referring to the September 11 attacks as "the greatest work of art one can imagine . . . the greatest work of art there is in the entire cosmos." *September 19, 2001*

—

"I know from personal experience how stereotypes can hurt, and I regret that my words could have conjured up an impression of Jewish 'control' of Hollywood. I sincerely apologize for my statement . . . which has been misinterpreted by a number of people."

Dolly Parton apologizing for telling a *Vogue* reporter that her idea for a TV series about a country singer who becomes a gospel singer after a near-death experience was rejected by Hollywood because "most of the people out here are Jewish, and it's a frightening thing for them to promote Christianity." *February 18, 1994*

—

"I offer no excuses for what happened. I made a terrible mistake. I got caught up in the excitement of the moment. I would never intentionally endanger the lives of my children."

Michael Jackson apologizing for holding—or, "dangling," as the media famously described it—his infant son Prince Michael II over the railing of a fourth-floor balcony so that fans crowded below his Berlin hotel suite could see the kid. *November 19, 2002*

⸺

"Whoever heard it and got bummed out, sorry."

Ozzy Osbourne guitarist Zakk Wylde apologizing for encouraging audience members at a New Year's Eve concert in Long Beach, CA, to beat up homosexuals. *January 5, 1989*

⸺

"I feel so bad. My band started playing the wrong song and I didn't know what to do so I thought I'd do a hoedown. I'm sorry."

Ashlee Simpson, apologizing after a career-defining humiliation on *Saturday Night Live* when she came out to perform her second song and the vocal track from the song she'd already sung started playing, thus exposing her as a lip-syncing fraud reduced to galumphing a little jig as she prematurely left the stage. *October 23, 2004*

⸺

"In the heat of the moment, I made a stupid remark. I apologize for it."

David Clayton-Thomas, lead singer for Blood, Sweat & Tears, apologizing for telling the audience in largely Jewish West Bloomfield, MI, that the weather was "as hot as the last train car going to Auschwitz." *July 25, 1995*

Forgive Me, Lord

"I apologize that, during a week when everyone appropriately dropped all labels and no one was seen as liberal or conservative, Democrat or Republican, religious or secular, I singled out for blame certain groups of Americans . . . This was insensitive, uncalled for at the time, and unnecessary as part of the commentary on this destruction. The only label any of us needs in such a terrible time of crisis is that of 'American.'"

Rev. Jerry Falwell apologizing for blaming groups "who have tried to secularize America"—"pagans" and "abortionists" and "feminists" and "gays" and "lesbians" and "the ACLU" and "People for the American Way"—for the September 11 attacks because they angered God enough to make Him "lift the curtain and allow the enemies of America to give us probably what we deserve . . . I point the finger in their face and say, 'You helped this happen.'" Though Pat Robertson, on whose *700 Club* TV show Falwell made these remarks, initially agreed with them ("I totally concur"), he wound up having to repudiate them as "totally inappropriate." *September 17, 2001*

—

"I sincerely apologize to anyone who was offended by my teasing."

Dr. Bailey Smith, president of the Southern Baptist Convention, apologizing for observing that Jews "got funny-looking noses." Smith—who had recently attracted attention with his declaration that "God almighty does not hear the prayer of a Jew, for how in the world can God hear the prayer of a man who says that Jesus Christ is not the true Messiah?"— was broadcasting a sermon over an Oklahoma City radio station when he said, "There are some people with whom God works more intimately than others. Why, you say? I don't know. Why did he choose the Jews? I don't know why he chose the Jews. I think they got funny-looking noses, myself. I don't know why he chose the Jews. That's God's business. Amen." After the transcript of the sermon was published in the *Dallas Morning News*, Smith said that he was not anti-Semitic, that it was "irresponsible for anyone to say that I am," and that the genesis of the unfortunate remark was an observation by "a handsome young Jewish man" who told him just before his sermon, "Preacher, you've got a bald spot and we Jews have funny noses." Explained Smith, "It was an aside. It wasn't part of my sermon. I was teasing as I talked to the people of my church. It was not a public meeting. Can't people tease any more at all?' *November 14, 1980*

—

"However innocent and unintended, it was insensitive and wrong. I affirm to you that the term was used in a private conversation . . . In private talks we sometimes let our guard down . . . It was not in a spirit of meanness. An off-color remark has no bearing on religion or politics. I denied and I do not recall ever making such a statement in any context

that would be remotely construed as being either remotely anti-Semitic or anti-Israel."

Rev. Jesse Jackson, candidate for the Democratic presidential nomination, apologizing at a Manchester, NH, temple for referring to Jews as "Hymie" and New York City as "Hymie-town." *February 26, 1984*

"If in my low moments in word, deed, or attitude, through some error of temper, taste, or tone, I have caused anyone discomfort, created pain, or revived someone's fears, that was not my truest self. If there were occasions when my grape turned into a raisin and my joy bell lost its resonance, please forgive me. Charge it to my head, so limited in its finitude, not to my heart, which is boundless in its love for the entire human family."

Rev. Jesse Jackson addressing the Democratic Convention in San Francisco, apologizing to the Jewish community for the aspects of his campaign it had a problem with: his failure to repudiate Rev. Louis Farrakhan (who referred to Judaism as either "a gutter religion" or, as he insisted he said, "a dirty religion," as if the distinction was significant) and of course the whole "Hymietown" thing—a controversy Jackson himself breathed new life into when he explained the origins of the phrase to *Newsweek*: "I think the first time I heard it was when I got to Chicago about twenty years ago. There's a place down off Maxwell Street called 'Jewtown.' Understand? 'Jewtown is where Hymie gets you if you can't negotiate them suits down,' you understand? That's not meant as anti-Semitic . . . If you can't buy any suits downtown, you go down to Jewtown on Maxwell Street, and you start negotiating with

Hyman and Sons . . . And if Hyman and Sons show up, they're called Hymie. There's no insult even to them." *July 17, 1984*

———

"Judgments were made regarding the assignment of John Geoghan which, in retrospect, were tragically incorrect."

Boston's Cardinal Bernard Law apologizing to the more than 130 people fondled or raped as children by Father John Geoghan for having known about Geoghan's child-molesting predilections and yet allowing him to continue as a priest. Cardinal Law resigned as archbishop almost a year later, after continuing revelations about his laissez-faire attitude regarding priests accused of sexual abuse. *January 9, 2002*

———

"We admit our mistake . . . Our church family humbly asks you to accept our apology."

Deacon Logan Lewis of the Barnetts Creek Baptist Church in Thomasville, GA, apologizing to Jaime L. Wireman and Jeffrey Johnson for having asked them to remove the coffin containing their one-day-old infant daughter Whitney Elaine from the church cemetery after the deacons discovered that Johnson was black. *March 29, 1996*

———

"If she doesn't remember that, I tell her I'm sorry. It was a terrible mistake and I believe Christ has forgiven me."

Jim Bakker, resigned head of the PTL TV ministry, insisting that despite former church secretary Jessica Hahn's claims that he never apologized for forcing her to have sex with him, he did in fact apologize to her two days after the encounter. Added Bakker about his and his wife's fall from grace, "If people can't forgive Jim and Tammy, then the whole world is doomed to hell." *June 23, 1987*

—

"I've tried to be a good priest but it's obvious I have failed and I accept responsibility."

Rev. John Cornelius apologizing in a statement read by a spokesman for the Seattle archdiocese that removed him from his post after a dozen men came forward and accused him of molesting them over the previous thirty years. *May 24, 2002*

—

"Let me assure you that we take this very seriously and are conducting a thorough investigation."

American Airlines CEO Gerard Arpey apologizing for the actions of pilot Rodger K. Findiesen, who got on the intercom before the start of a Los Angeles–to–New York flight not to update passengers about the trip but rather to announce that more than half of Americans are Christians, and to invite Christian passengers to identify themselves. "You can use your time wisely on this flight," he told them, "or you can sit back and watch the movie." A wise use of time would presumably have been to try to convert the likes of passenger Amanda Nelligan, who said of the pilot's proselytizing, "I was definitely made to feel nervous, as were a lot of the people around me." *February 12, 2004*

—

"I offer my sincere, personal apologies for my failure to take firm and decisive action much earlier. If I have caused you or your parishioners additional grief by my handling of the Baker case, I ask your forgiveness."

Cardinal Roger M. Mahony apologizing in a letter to the Catholic Archdiocese of Los Angeles for allowing child-molesting priest Michael Baker to continue to serve in various ministries despite the fact that "in late 1986, Baker disclosed to me that he had problems in the past of acting out sexually with two minors." *May 14, 2002*

—

"I sincerely apologize that certain statements of mine made during an interview for the Sept. 30 edition of CBS's *60 Minutes* were hurtful to the feelings of many Muslims. I intended no disrespect to any sincere, law-abiding Muslim."

Rev. Jerry Falwell apologizing for saying, "I think Muhammad was a terrorist." *October 12, 2002*

—

"I am responsible and I apologize for my conduct. It is my problem. There is no relation of this to the church or any other group."

Mormon Church spokesman Lloyd Gerald Pond, a vociferous denouncer of sexual abuse, apologizing and resigning after pleading guilty to forcing a fourteen-year-old girl to fellate him. *November 22, 1996*

—

"Since the night of June fourteenth, I have had a heavy heart and have had a lot of agony for what I did to the Afro-

American community by the allegations I made to the police. I apologize to all in the Afro-American community. I want to make amends."

Rev. Thomas Spisak apologizing for claiming that two black men attacked him in his Warren, OH, church residence when, in fact, he had stabbed himself eighty-eight times in a failed suicide attempt. *January 28, 1999*

⸺

"I am appalled by the things that have resulted from the actions of my father and others in that cult. I am deeply hurt by the knowledge that people have now lost their lives in connection with my father. My sympathy and prayers go out to all those who are suffering the loss of loved ones."

Mark Applewhite, son of Heaven's Gate leader Marshall Applewhite, apologizing to the relatives of the thirty-eight doomsday cult members who joined his father in a mass suicide, believing that the visibility of the Hale-Bopp comet heralded the arrival of the spaceship that would transport them from their beds in a mansion near San Diego—where they all were dressed in black exercise outfits accessorized with diamond-shaped purple shrouds—to heaven. *March 29, 1997*

⸺

"I never realized this would cause such a fuss. To read the papers, you would think that I'm not a very nice man. There are a number of people who have been repulsed by my illustration of a modern-day parable with this gimmick. I publicly ask any that I have offended to forgive me. Because people may be turned away from God through the use of this device, I have discontinued its use. **The famous little wood chair has been eliminated from our plans."**

Rev. Dwight Wymer of Immanuel Baptist Church in Grand Rapids, MI, apologizing for hooking up a six-volt battery to a wire-covered stool as a teaching tool in his Bible class. "I am a pastor who is willing to utilize many gimmicks to catch the attention of people to hear the word of God. This gimmick's purpose was to gain the attention and hold the interest of the group and was used only for this purpose," he said, pointing out that his makeshift electric chair "was used for only one illustration during the twelve-and-a-half hours of teaching time the children received." Said Terri TenHopen, whose eight-year-old son was photographed receiving the single shock administered, "I don't think Bryan learned a thing about God by sitting on that seat. The only thing he learned was not to sit there again." *July 12, 1981*

—

"I do not plan in any way to whitewash my sin or call it a mistake. I call it a sin. I beg your forgiveness."

Jimmy Swaggart apologizing to his Baton Rouge, LA, congregation for doing something bad. He didn't say what specifically, but it seemed to have something to do with recently surfaced photos of him going into a motel room with a prostitute. *February 21, 1988*

—

"God never gave a man a better helpmate, a companion to stand beside him. I have sinned against you and I beg your forgiveness."

Jimmy Swaggart apologizing to his wife. *February 21, 1988*

===

"To my fellow television evangelists, already bearing an almost unbearable burden, I have made your load heavier and I have hurt you. Please, please, forgive me."

Jimmy Swaggart apologizing to his colleagues as he gave up his own ministry "for an undetermined, indeterminate period of time." *February 21, 1988*

===

"I have sinned against Thee, O Lord, and I ask that your precious blood would wash and cleanse me until it is in the seas of God's forgiveness, never to be remembered anymore."

Jimmy Swaggart apologizing to God. *February 21, 1988*

===

"The university does not encourage this type of action and will use its best efforts to see that is not repeated."

Rev. Bill Shuler, Oral Roberts University's pastor, apologizing to the Islamic Society of Tulsa, OK, for an incident in which upward of twenty ORU students surrounded a local mosque, laid their hands on it, and prayed. *February 7, 1997*

===

"This is no time for evasions, denials, or alibis. No doubt, many close friends and supporters will be disappointed in me. I ask for their forgiveness, understanding, and prayers. I will be taking some time off to revive my spirit and reconnect with my family before I return to my public ministry."

Rev. Jesse Jackson apologizing for having fathered a then-twenty-month-old daughter with a woman who worked for his Rainbow/PUSH Coalition. Sweetest detail: Karin L. Stanford was pregnant with Jackson's child during the period of time that Jackson was advising Bill Clinton about how to weather the Monica Lewinsky scandal. *January 18, 2001*

——

"I am aware that certain remarks made during my recent deposition have received widespread attention and that people have found them hurtful. For this I am sorry and I apologize."

Rev. William Loyens apologizing for suggesting that the abuse of Alaskan boys by a Jesuit priest was less damaging than priestly abuse of other American boys because the native Alaskan culture was "fairly loose" about sex. *March 15, 2004*

——

"I apologize to each one of you immensely."

Bishop Charles Grahmann apologizing to eleven former altar boys (one of whom committed suicide years earlier) after a jury ordered the Catholic Diocese of Dallas to pay them close to $120 million in damages for ignoring repeated complaints about the hundreds of instances of sexual abuse they were subjected to by former Dallas priest Rudolph Kos. *July 27, 1997*

——

"It's a humorous statement that doesn't mean anything. You can't lie to God—it's ridiculous. If it's an insult, I certainly didn't think it was, but if they are offended, then I certainly offer an apology."

Televangelist Jimmy Swaggart apologizing for saying, "I've never seen a man in my life I wanted to marry. And I'm going to be blunt and plain: if one ever looks at me like that, I'm going to kill him and tell God he died." *September 22, 2004*

⸺

"As the author of *The Satanic Verses*, I recognize that Moslems in many parts of the world are genuinely distressed by the publication of my novel. I profoundly regret the distress the publication has occasioned to sincere followers of Islam. Living as we do in a world of many faiths, this experience has served to remind us that we must all be conscious of the sensibilities of others."

Author Salman Rushdie apologizing, or, at the very least, expressing regret, for offending Muslims so much with his book—by suggesting that the prophet Muhammad (and not God) wrote the Koran and by depicting his wives as prostitutes—that Iran's Ayatollah Khomeini issued a fatwa calling on followers of Islam to assassinate him. *February 18, 1989*

⸺

"Early in the flight I should have tried harder to be more polite and later I absolutely should not have aggressively grabbed his shoulders or touched him in any way . . . My intent was to get his attention, not to cause physical harm. Nevertheless, my actions were inappropriate, considering the circumstances, and wherever he might be, I want him to know that I apologize for any portion of my conduct which he found offensive . . . I know that this incident caused others to be inconvenienced. As a result, I wish to express an apology to all other members of the flight crew and passengers, who were delayed or otherwise disrupted because of these events."

Garden Grove, CA, televangelist Rev. Robert H. Schuller apologizing in a Brooklyn courtroom for laying his hands on a United Airlines flight attendant who first refused to let him hang up a garment bag containing his clerical robe and then wouldn't serve him grapes without the cheese they normally came with. No one asked, "Hey, Reverend, why didn't you just *not eat the cheese?*" *August 13, 1997*

—

"Is it right to call for assassination? No, and I apologize for that statement."

Pat Robertson apologizing for calling for the assassination of Venezuelan president Hugo Chavez and then denying having said it even as the footage of exactly what he'd said ("If he thinks we're trying to assassinate him, I think that we really ought to go ahead and do it. It's a whole lot cheaper than starting a war") was all over the Internet. *August 24, 2005*

—

"I had scores of conversations with Mr. Nixon in which we discussed every conceivable subject. However, I cannot imagine what caused me to make those comments, which I totally repudiate. Whatever the reason, I was wrong for not disagreeing with the President, and I sincerely apologize to anyone I have offended. I don't ever recall having those feelings about any group, especially the Jews, and I certainly do not have them now. My remarks did not reflect my love for the Jewish people. I humbly ask the Jewish community to reflect on my actions on behalf of Jews over the years that contradict my words in the Oval Office that day."

Rev. Billy Graham apologizing for anti-Semitic comments in a 1972 conversation that was part of five hundred hours of Nixon tapes released by the National Archives. One highlight: Graham agreeing with Nixon that left-wing Jews run the media. "They're the ones putting out the pornographic stuff. This stranglehold has got to be broken or this country's going down the drain," to which Nixon responded, "You believe that? . . . Oh boy. So do I. I can't ever say that but I believe it." Graham also said, "A lot of Jews are great friends of mine. They swarm around me and are friendly to me. Because they know that I am friendly to Israel and so forth. But they don't know how I really feel about what they're doing to this country," to which Nixon responded, "You must not let them know." *March 16, 2002*

=

"I apologize to my Jewish friends here and around the world and I apologize to the Christians here for having created any kind of rift . . . I apologize not for what I believe, but for my lack of tact and judgment in making a statement that served no purpose whatsoever."
Rev. Jerry Falwell apologizing for telling an evangelical conference that the Antichrist—the biblical figure promoting the wave of evil that will precede Christ's Second Coming—is a contemporary Jewish man. "If he's going to be the counterfeit of Christ, he has to be Jewish," Falwell said. "The only thing we know is he must be male and Jewish." *February 2, 1999*

Politically Incorrect

"I want to say to you, yes, that I have behaved badly sometimes. Yes, it is true that I was on rowdy movie sets and I have done things that were not right which I thought then was playful but now I recognize that I have offended people. And to those people that I have offended, I want to say to them I am deeply sorry about that and I apologize because this is not what I'm trying to do."

California gubernatorial candidate Arnold Schwarzenegger (R) apologizing after a *Los Angeles Times* article documented the allegations by six women of sexual harassment and groping over the past three decades. Though his apology tried to make it seem as if his beyond-boorish behavior was confined to "rowdy movie sets," most of the offenses described occurred far from the klieg lights: breasts were grabbed in a gym, a hotel room, an elevator, and on a public street, a buttock was grabbed in a production office, and an astonishingly lewd request was made to a waitress in a coffee shop. *October 2, 2003*

"I apologize, but I don't think I had the gay vote anyway."

Houston mayoral candidate Louie Welch apologizing for saying on TV, in a remark not intended for an open microphone, that among his four-point plan to stop the spread of

AIDS, "One of them is to shoot the queers." Said his opponent, Mayor Kathy Whitmire, "It would be hard to understand
why a mayoral candidate would say something like that." One
possible clue: Welch raised over $69,000 in one day after his
"gaffe." *October 24, 1985*

**"I'm sure I've hurt some people in Washington. I'm sure
I've embarrassed some people. I've caused some pain
among people in this city . . . And to those people I offer my
deepest and sincere apologies, my sincere regrets and my
feeling of remorse about it."**

Washington, D.C., mayor Marion Barry (D) apologizing for
getting arrested for cocaine possession at the Vista Hotel,
where he was videotaped smoking crack. "Bitch set me up,"
Barry said, referring to his longtime friend Hazel Moore, who
lured him there and offered him the pipe. "This goddamn
bitch, setting me up like this. Set me up, ain't that a bitch . . .
goddamn bitch." *March 14, 1990*

**"I want to sincerely apologize to you personally for the
shame I have brought to the mayor's office and the city and
the embarrassment my lack of judgment may cause you."**

Spokane, WA, mayor Jim West (R), whose previous stint in
the state legislature was notable for his antigay agenda, apologizing for offering a City Hall internship as an enticement
to an Internet acquaintance he believed to be an eighteen-
year-old gay man but was actually an employee of a local
newspaper investigating him. "The Gay.com thing has only
been, I can't recall, but it hasn't been very long," West told the

Spokesman-Review as he denied allegations of decades-old pedophilia with Boy Scouts. "I can't tell you why I go there, to tell you the truth . . . curiosity, confused, whatever, I don't know." Still, he said, "I wouldn't characterize me as 'gay.'" *May 5, 2005*

"I reject categorically racial hatred. My politics in this House will be on a high plane. I call for equal rights, for non-discrimination. I'm deeply sorry for the embarrassment this may have caused you."

Former grand wizard of the Ku Klux Klan and current Louisiana state representative David Duke apologizing for getting himself photographed shaking hands with Art Jones, the vice chairman of the American Nazi Party. "Because of my controversial background, the media saw it as an opportunity to discredit me," he said, clearly feeling sorry for himself as he explained that it was only after he'd shaken hands with Jones that he realized he was dealing with "a Nazi kook. My heart sank at that moment. I was powerless to prevent the assassination of my character." Then, positively preening in his self-pity, he added, "I guess when I'm ninety years old, they'll be calling me an ex–Klan wizard." *March 6, 1989*

"I am very sorry if I caused any offense or embarrassment to anyone. It was a poor choice of costume and I apologize."

Britain's Prince Harry apologizing for wearing a Nazi uniform, complete with swastika armband, to a friend's birthday party. *January 12, 2005*

"I feel terrible that my criticism of NBC for airing this movie has been misinterpreted as a criticism of *Schindler's List*, or the millions of Jews who died senselessly during the Holocaust. To all those that I've offended, I offer an apology. And I personally apologize for appearing insensitive to the worst atrocities known to humankind."

Rep. Tom Coburn (R-OK), head of the Congressional Family Caucus, apologizing for accusing NBC of taking network television "to an all-time low, with full-frontal nudity, violence and profanity" by honoring its contract and airing Steven Spielberg's film uncut. To Coburn's surprise, his assumption that "decent-minded individuals everywhere" would be outraged was way off the mark, as even the most fervent moral scolds distanced themselves from his crusade. William Bennett, author of *The Book of Virtues*, called Coburn's position "very unfortunate and foolish," since it "obscures, even obliterates, the distinction between gratuitous violence and nudity—that is violence and nudity to titillate—and violence and human realism essential to the telling of an important story or historical truth," with Sen. Alfonse D'Amato (R-NY) chiming in that "to equate the nudity of Holocaust victims in the concentration camps with any sexual connotation is outrageous and offensive." And this from Rep. Mark Foley (R-FL): "He complained about nudity. These people's clothes were stolen. Violence? These people were murdered." *February 26, 1997*

"If I offended Arab Americans, I regret my choice of words."

Rep. John Cooksey (R-LA) apologizing for saying of increased airport security, "If I see someone come in and he's got a diaper on his head and a fan belt around that diaper on his head, that guy needs to be pulled over and checked." He explained that the diaper-topped "man I had on my mind was Osama bin Laden and I never intended to disparage loyal Americans of Arab descent," adding that we can't win a war on terrorism "if we have to stop every five minutes to make sure we're being politically correct." *September 20, 2001*

"It was meant to be a prank and it turned out to be more serious than it was intended. It all certainly was in bad taste. That type of act is certainly not condoned by anyone in this House."

Texas House Speaker Gib Lewis apologizing for the inappropriate greeting arranged by House colleagues to help Rep. David Patronella (D-Houston) celebrate his twenty-sixth birthday—a blond stripper bumping and grinding down to her G-string and pasties, mere millimeters in front of Patronella's smiling face, in a public lobby of the state capitol building. *May 12, 1983*

"I was raised and taught and believe the people of Israel to be God's chosen and special people. I have studied history and have great respect and regard for the business success of the Jewish people. My remark was issued out of respect for this people and not out of disrespect. However, I apologize to anyone who was offended by this remark."

Gov. Guy Hunt (R-AL) apologizing for saying that he "never tried to Jew" a peach farmer to get a lower price on fruit. "It's not an ethnic slur," he explained. "You don't make an ethnic slur before several hundred people. There's nothing in my background and beliefs that would make it an ethnic slur." *June 29, 1987*

—

"I immediately apologized to her and I want to do so again for the misunderstanding."

California education secretary Richard Riordan apologizing for a bizarre exchange at the Santa Barbara Central Library with a preschooler who told him her name was Isis and asked if he knew that meant "Egyptian goddess," at which point Riordan, thinking she was asking if he knew what her name meant (and thinking he had a pretty darn hilarious rejoinder) blurted, "Stupid dirty girl." (At which point, according to a witness, little Isis matter-of-factly corrected him.) *July 2, 2004*

—

"This is the first time my desire to put a spin on events has crossed the line from an honest discussion of my views to an exaggeration that turned out to be inaccurate. I went too far. My remarks left the impression of something that was not true and did not occur."

Ed Rollins, chief strategist for New Jersey Republican governor-elect Christine Todd Whitman, apologizing for saying that the campaign had spent some $500,000 to suppress the black vote. Tactics that he actually boasted about included going "into the black churches" and offering financial rewards if preachers would refrain from encouraging a large urban turnout, and approaching urban Democrats hired to get out the vote and saying to them, "How much have they paid you to do your normal duty? We'll match it. Go home, sit and watch television." *November 10, 1993*

—

"When I make a mistake, it's a beaut. There's no question this was a mistake. I had no intention of offending anyone."

Sen. Robert F. Bennett (R-UT) apologizing to his state's NAACP for declaring that the only thing that could keep George W. Bush from being the Republican nominee in 2000 would be if "he was hit by a bus or some woman comes forward, let's say some black woman comes forward with an illegitimate child that he fathered within the last eighteen months." He explained that he'd been thinking about events in the movie *Primary Colors*. *August 23, 1999*

—

"We're sorry if this joke, which got a lot of laughs, offended anyone."

David Young, manager of the reelection campaign of Sen. Jim Bunning (R-KY), apologizing for the senator's observation that his likely Democratic opponent, state senator Daniel Mongiardo, "looks like one of Saddam Hussein's sons . . . I mean before they were dead, of course . . . And he even dresses like them, too." *March 31, 2004*

—

"I deeply regret having related a story from the campaign trail which could have been interpreted that I share racist views. Such views are inappropriate and belong in the past and that was the context in which the story was told. But

more importantly, they are views which I do not condone and do not share."

Sen. Conrad Burns (R-MT) apologizing for relating verbatim a question posed to him by an elderly constituent ("Conrad, how can you live back there [in Washington, D.C.] with all those niggers?") and for his chuckling response ("I said, 'It's a hell of a challenge'"). Asked why he hadn't instead told the man he disapproved of racial slurs, he said, "I don't know, I never give it much thought." *October 20, 1994*

⸺

"I used the word 'niggardly' in reference to my administration of a fund. Although the word, which is defined as miserly, does not have any racial connotations, I realize that staff members present were offended by the word. I immediately apologized . . . I would never think of making a racist remark."

David Howard (white), an aide to Washington, D.C., mayor Anthony A. Williams (black), apologizing for using a word correctly. Howard actually felt compelled to resign—and Williams to accept his resignation—over this silliness, and sporting goods store worker Marcus Marshall (black) saw a certain justice in this, saying, "I don't agree with him saying that kind of word. He should be punished because it's so close to . . . a degrading word." It took the mayor a week to come to his senses and hire Howard back. *January 26, 1999*

⸺

"If I offended anyone, I apologize. I don't think in twenty-one years I have ever made an offensive remark knowingly."

Savannah, GA's five-term Democratic mayor John Rousakis

apologizing for making a joke about a rape victim who couldn't identify her attacker but knew he was a Democrat because she "never had it so good." *April 29, 1991*

—

"I feel just terrible about this. I had no intention in my heart to hurt anyone, especially those women who have been traumatized by rape. Looking back, I realize it was insensitive and had no place at the campfire or in any setting."

Texas gubernatorial nominee Clayton Williams (R) apologizing "from the bottom of my heart" for comparing his having to endure inclement weather on his ranch to a woman being raped: "If it's inevitable, just relax and enjoy it." *March 25, 1990*

—

"We all know in the heat of debate that things are said without careful thought as to precise meaning or implication. I never intended nor meant to infer that consensual sexual acts between adults of the same sex are in the same category as violent sexual acts. I regret that I made the statement."

State senator Al Bishop (R-MT) apologizing for describing gay sex as "even worse than" rape. *March 23, 1995*

—

"I apologize deeply for the thoughtless and insensitive remark. Sexual harassment in the workplace is a most demeaning problem for anyone to suffer."

State senator Steven Casey (D-CT) apologizing for declaring, in the middle of debate on a bill that would ban such harassment, "I wish *I* were sexually harassed." *April 16, 1980*

—

"If I offended anyone, I'm sorry. I was making fun of the pomposity of the judge and the manner in which he's dragging the trial out."

Sen. Alfonse D'Amato (R-NY), upset because the O. J. Simpson trial was distracting people from things he thought they might be better off paying attention to (like the Whitewater hearings he was eager to begin), apologizing via fax for using a crude accent to make fun of Japanese American judge Lance Ito on the nationally syndicated Don Imus radio show. "Judge Ito will never let it end," D'Amato said in his pidgin Japanese American accent. "Judge Ito loves the limelight. He is making a disgrace of the judicial system, little Judge Ito." *April 5, 1995*

━

"It was a poor attempt at humor, and I have great respect for the Congressman, and I was wrong. And I apologize to him."

Sen. Alfonse D'Amato (R-NY) apologizing for making fun of the weight of Rep. Jerrold L. Nadler (D-NY) by referring to him as "Jerry Waddler," while expressing no regrets for calling his election opponent, Rep. Charles E. Schumer, a "putzhead"—an insult he at first denied ("I have no knowledge of it. Certainly never in a public domain . . . I have not engaged in that. I wouldn't engage in it. It's wrong. I haven't done it") and then admitted while justifying it as having been uttered not publicly but at a "private meeting." Said former New York governor Mario Cuomo, "To think that he makes that confession—'We would never say putzhead . . . where we could get caught and everybody might get angry.'" Schumer's victory two weeks later ended D'Amato's eighteen-year Senate run. *October 22, 1998*

—

"I want to apologize for the inappropriate and insensitive treatment several of the participants were subjected to at the entrance gate of the White House. It was wrong . . . I deeply regret any insult or embarrassment you suffered."

President Bill Clinton apologizing to about fifty gay politicians who arrived at the White House for a meeting and were greeted by Secret Service agents wearing rubber gloves. *June 19, 1995*

—

"I made a very unfortunate and insensitive remark. It was the wrong thing to do, and I have no excuse for it."

Sen. John McCain (R-AZ) apologizing to the *Washington Post* for saying at a Republican fund-raiser that the reason Chelsea Clinton is "so ugly" is that "she's the child of Janet Reno and Hillary Clinton." Though he sent a personal note to the Clintons, he saw no reason to apologize to Reno. *June 11, 1998*

—

"I waited a long time to be able to express to the country how very sorry I am for my part in the past year's ordeal. And, of course, I've—I've apologized in private to my family and to my friends that I would like to publicly acknowledge the pain and the suffering that they've gone through because of this. I wouldn't dream of asking Chelsea and Mrs. Clinton to forgive me, but I would ask them to know that I am very sorry for what happened and for what they've been through."

Monica Lewinsky during an interview with ABC's Barbara

Walters, apologizing for everything that happened after she
flashed her thong at her "sexual soul mate," Bill Clinton.
March 3, 1999

———

**"It was an unfortunate remark that once it's in print it looks
a lot worse than it actually is."**
Sen. Bob Kerrey (D-NE) apologizing for saying of his former
rival for the presidency, "Clinton's an unusually good liar.
Unusually good. Do you realize that?" *February 6, 1996*

———

**"I'm very sorry I did that. You were all yelling at my
husband, whom I love. I apologize, but it will not rid the
anger in my heart. My brother is dying and he grows thinner
every day and has sores on his body . . . I want you to understand there's great anger and pain inside of me."**
Sally Dornan apologizing for blurting out, "Shut up, fag!" at
a gay activist who was attacking Rep. Robert Dornan (R-CA)
at a town meeting, explaining that she was very upset about
her brother's case of AIDS. Rep. Dornan, who knew he had a
gay brother-in-law, didn't know the man was dying of AIDS.
"Why didn't you tell me?" he asked his wife, who replied, "I
didn't want to hurt you." *September 18, 1988*

———

**"[My wife] and I deeply regret our actions with our personal
checking account. Despite the fact that we were told that
holding checks was standing operating procedure, and
despite the fact that no taxpayer's money was involved, we
should have known better. We should not have been so**

casual and careless with our personal account. We are sorry and apologize."

Rep. Gerry Sikorski (D-MN) apologizing for being one of the main offenders in the House of Representatives' check-kiting scandal, having written 697 bad checks totaling over $120,000. *March 13, 1992*

———

"I regret the errors with my checking account and apologize for them. But one thing I do not apologize for is leading the fight for disclosure of all the names. Last year and last month the Democratic leadership tried to suppress the facts. I fought for disclosure even though I knew I would be opening myself to public embarrassment."

House Minority Whip Newt Gingrich (R-GA) apologizing for bouncing twenty-two checks totaling almost $27,000. *April 16, 1992*

———

"I in no way intended those remarks to be a comment on Hispanics or Mexican Americans. I apologize for my choice of words, if they offended anyone."

Presidential nomination seeker Sen. Ernest "Fritz" Hollings (D-SC) apologizing for referring to the Alan Cranston supporters present in Iowa as "wetbacks from California." Explained his Iowa campaign manager, Ken Purcell, Hollings "did not mean it in a racial sense. It was meant in the sense of people crossing a state border to do something in another state. I hope people will not take it as a racial insult. It was not meant as such." *October 12, 1983*

———

"My remark was a mistake, as it used a term which I under-stand is not acceptable today. All I can do now in respect to the incident is to say that I am very sorry and hope that people of good will accept my sincere apologies."

La Quinta, CA, mayor Robert Baier apologizing for saying, at a news conference the day after his election, "We have more wetbacks around here than you can shake a stick at." Said Baier, "This was my first and only such remark that could be deemed a racial slur and I know that most of us have made a mistake in our lifetime." *April 19, 1983*

"I regret the use of such an inappropriate term. I hope I did not overshadow the serious substance of my remarks."

Sen. Conrad Burns (R-MT) apologizing for a speech about U.S. dependence on foreign oil in which he referred to Arabs as "ragheads." *March 11, 1999*

"It was off-the-cuff and in jest, and that's stupid when you're in public life, and I should know better."

Maryland governor Robert Ehrlich's wife, Kendel, apolo-gizing for saying, in the course of a discussion about the diffi-culties of raising girls in a culture riddled with sexual imagery, "You know, really, if I had an opportunity to shoot Britney Spears, I think I would." *October 8, 2003*

"Some of my friends have asked me why did I do something so dumb? The best answer I can give is that this was a very difficult time in my life. Dealing with being gay, while continuing to meet my public obligations, created tremendous internal pressures. Those pressures ended when I spoke publicly about my own personal identity. Not coincidentally, my judgment has improved since then . . . I hope you will accept my apology."

Rep. Barney Frank (D-MA) apologizing in a letter to supporters for his involvement with Stephen L. Gobie, who ran a prostitution ring out of Frank's Capitol Hill apartment. The House officially reprimanded Frank several months later. *September 22, 1989*

━

"The media and others are reporting this as if it were intentional, and it was not. I repeat, this was nothing more than the unintentional mispronunciation of another person's name that sounded like it was something that it was not."

House Republican leader Dick Armey (R-TX) excusing himself more than apologizing for referring to Rep. Barney Frank as "Barney Fag." Armey, protesting too much, said, "I do not want Barney Frank to believe for one moment I would use a slur against him. I had a trouble with alliteration. I was stumbling, mumbling . . . Barney Frank is a friend of mine. I don't use the word in personal conversation. I would not use such an expression and I don't approve of anyone who does this." Responded the openly gay Frank, "There are various ways to mispronounce my name, but that one, I think, is the least common." And, as his mother put it, "In the fifty-nine years since I married your father, no one has ever called me Elsie Fag." Armey's bizarre obsession with Frank surfaced again five years later, when he said, "I am Dick Armey. And if there is a dick army, Barney Frank would want to join up." *January 27, 1995*

⸺

"I shouldn't have repeated the story. It was inappropriate and I apologize for doing so."

Sen. John Kerry (D-MA) apologizing for his joking response to a question at a businesspeople's breakfast about Vice President–elect Dan Quayle's qualifications: "The Secret Service is under orders that if Bush is shot, to shoot Quayle." Then, in keeping with his have-it-both-ways personality, he added, "Now, folks, I don't mean that. I'm just relating what some people are saying in Washington." *November 16, 1988*

⸺

"If I could change places with him, I would. It's easy for me to say that, but I would. All I can say, Judge, is I'm sorry for what happened and I wish I could change it."

Resigned representative Bill Janklow (R-SD) apologizing after being sentenced to one hundred days in jail for second-degree manslaughter. Janklow, who never interpreted the more than a dozen speeding tickets he received in recent years (or the eight accidents he had, or the close call he'd had eight months earlier at the same intersection) as any kind of warning to drive more carefully, ran a Stop sign and plowed into motorcyclist Randy Scott at over seventy miles per hour. *January 22, 2004*

⸺

"The entire city is entitled to my apology and I want to give it at this time. I can only say to you, I'm truly sorry for the problems my actions have caused."

Houston city councilman Jim Westmoreland apologizing for suggesting to a reporter that, in order to satisfy blacks who wanted to rename a Houston airport in honor of the late Rep. Mickey Leland (D-TX), the airport should instead be renamed "Nigger International." *November 1, 1989*

—

"Let me say to the entire House that two years ago, when I became the first Republican speaker in forty years, to the degree I was too brash, too self-confident or too pushy, I apologize. To whatever degree, in any way that I brought controversy or inappropriate attention to the House, I apologize . . . Some of this difficulty, frankly, I brought on myself . . . And I apologize to the House and the country for having done so."

House Speaker Newt Gingrich apologizing for various ethics violations and for, basically, his personality. *January 7, 1997*

—

"I owe my wife, Eileen, President Clinton, Vice President Gore and my colleagues in the White House a public apology. I took every manner of security precautions when I joined the President. But then I talked to a prostitute at night. What was I thinking? I wasn't thinking. I was in blind denial, out of control, driven by my ego. I could not bring myself to imagine the consequences of what I was doing. To do so would be to admit that I would have to curb my behavior. Anything but that!"

Former White House advisor Dick Morris apologizing in his memoir, *Behind the Oval Office*, for his relationship with prostitute Sherry Rowlands, during which he allowed her to listen in on his conversations with Clinton. The apology wasn't enough for Eileen, who divorced him. *January 15, 1997*

—

"They were gestures of friendship to two friends, political equals, and I certainly meant no disrespect or offense. If I had offended anyone, I was sorry and it hasn't happened again nor will it."

Canadian prime minister John Turner in the midst of his reelection campaign, apologizing—after laughingly dismissing the incidents as evidence that he was a "tactile politician"—for patting the backsides of two female political associates. The liberal Turner was defeated by conservative Brian Mulroney a month later. *August 13, 1984*

⸻

"I humbly want to apologize if the e-mail forwarded from my office on Monday night was offensive or disrespectful to any one in this General Assembly, state or nation . . . I am not now nor have I ever been a racist or white supremacist."

State legislator Don Davis (R-NC) apologizing for forwarding (to every one of his colleagues) an e-mail declaring, "Two things made this country great: White men & Christianity." Claiming that the e-mail "was not intended to be indicative of my personal views," Davis explained that his sole purpose in sending this rather provocative message was "to show the type of messages that come across the Internet." *August 22, 2001*

⸻

"I am very much hurt if I brought hurt to anyone because of that mistake. I apologize for any hurt that I brought to anybody."

Ultraconservative representative Robert Dornan (R-CA) apologizing for referring to Soviet news commentator Vladimir Posner, who appeared on ABC to provide commentary on a national security speech by President Ronald Reagan, as "a disloyal, betraying little Jew." Dornan explained, "I was not even aware that those words had come together in my sentence." *February 28, 1986*

———

"My conduct that evening was inappropriate . . . It violated the values of the person I strive to be."
Rep. Ken Calvert (R-CA) apologizing for being caught in "an extremely embarrassing situation"—sitting in a parked car in Riverside County getting a blowjob from a prostitute. His explanation: he had no idea that the woman was a prostitute (though he picked her up on a street frequented by prostitutes) and he didn't pay her (probably because he got arrested before he could) and so he didn't do anything illegal after all. *April 26, 1994*

———

"If I offended Betsy or anyone, I'm terribly sorry."
Peter Freyne, press secretary for Vermont governor Madeleine Kunin (D), apologizing for responding to a question by reporter Betsy Liley by saying, "If you took off all your clothes and [performed a lewd act], I might tell you." He resigned days later. *February 21, 1990*

———

"I'm sorry—so, so sorry that mistakes in my judgment made this day necessary for us all. I'm sorry that my actions have hurt those I love, in my personal and political lives. And I am sorry that I disappointed the citizens . . . who gave me enormous trust. To be clear, I am not apologizing for

being a gay American, but rather for having let personal feelings impact my decision making, and for not having the courage to be open about whom I was."

Gov. James E. McGreevey (D-NJ), having announced his intention to resign because he had an extramarital affair with a man who he then appointed as a homeland security adviser (and who then demanded five million dollars to stay silent), apologizing to his constituents a week before he left office. *November 8, 2004*

"The men and women of the San Diego Police Department do not deserve this type of language, and I apologize."

San Diego city manager Sylvester Murray apologizing for saying that, given his background as a Miami ghetto youth to whom the police were the enemy, being the "boss of police" now gives him an "orgasm." *June 5, 1986*

"I'm so sorry, I didn't mean it."

Nancy Reagan apologizing for telling her husband, in a phone call heard over loudspeakers at a Chicago campaign rally, that she wished he could have been there to see "all these beautiful white people." Realizing her faux pas, she added, "beautiful black and white people," though there were no blacks in attendance. State representative Donald Totten, Reagan's Illinois campaign director, later explained, "She was talking to her husband about the white snow [he was looking at in New Hampshire], and that's how she got mixed up." *February 16, 1980*

"No slur was intended and I apologize to anyone who was offended by it."

Ronald Reagan apologizing for telling this joke while campaigning in New Hampshire: "How do you tell the Polish one at a cockfight? He's the one with the duck. How do you tell the Italian? He's the one who bets on the duck. How do you tell when the Mafia's there? The duck wins." Reagan later explained that he doesn't "like that type of humor," and that the only reason he told it was to give an example of the kind of jokes he disapproves of. *February 18, 1980*

"I deeply regret any harm that I've done. I am grateful to the president for this second chance to get on with the job that the American people sent President Reagan here to do."

Budget director David A. Stockman thanking his boss for not firing him and apologizing for "my poor judgment and loose talk," as demonstrated in a series of interviews he gave reporter William Greider for an article in the *Atlantic Monthly* about Reagan's economic policies and Stockman's private belief—contrary to his public statements—that they would lead to huge budget deficits. Key Stockman quote: "None of us understands what's going on with all these numbers." *November 12, 1981*

"I'm sorry. I made a mistake."

Sen. Bob Packwood (R-OR) in a tense phone call to President Ronald Reagan, apologizing for telling the Associated Press that congressional Republicans "just shake our heads" at Reagan's frequently inappropriate responses to their concerns. As an example, he described how the efforts of Senate Budget Chairman Pete Domenici (R-NM) to discuss the $120 billion budget deficit were met with this presidential anecdote: "You know, a young man went into a grocery store and he had an orange in one hand and a bottle of vodka in the other, and he paid for the orange with food stamps, and he took the change and paid for the vodka. That's what's wrong." *March 2, 1982*

—

"My choice of words about the coal leasing commission today was unfortunate. I have apologized to the one member of the commission who is handicapped. I remain very proud of the commission, which is made up of highly talented people, reflecting a broad cross-section of our population."

Interior Secretary James Watt, who had previously coughed up apologies to Jewish liberals (whose opposition to his environmental policies he claimed threatened "our ability to be a good friend of Israel"), American Indians (whose reservations he said were examples of "the failures of socialism"), and the Beach Boys (whose crazy rock music attracted "the wrong element"), apologizing now for boasting of the diversity of his advisory group with the immortal phrase, "We have every kind of mixture you can have. I have a black, I have a woman, two Jews and a cripple." His resignation followed days later. *September 21, 1983*

—

"I freely apologize to anyone I have harmed by my taping practices. I very much regret any embarrassment the recent

revelations may have caused them . . . I used recording equipment in the way others use written notes—to help me make more fully informed decisions and to convey these decisions to associates more effectively. My purpose was always to extend the reach of my own memory, never to threaten or humiliate others. But it has become quite clear to me that in trying to be meticulous about my own managerial tasks I frequently ignored the potential impact on others. I now understand that taping of others without their consent is unfair, invades their privacy, and can lead to other more dangerous practices . . . I am sorry for my insensitivity in engaging in this practice and I hope all the current public attention will lead other government officials to behave more thoughtfully than I did."

U.S. Information Agency director Charles Z. Wick apologizing for surreptitiously recording phone conversations (after denying it for days). "Look," he told reporters, "I did a very dumb thing, and now I can see that and it's painful. But what else can I do but apologize to anybody I've offended?" *January 9, 1984*

"I sincerely regret the oversight and apologize to the committee."

White House counselor and Attorney General–designate Edwin Meese III apologizing in a letter to Senate Judiciary Committee chairman Strom Thurmond (R-SC) for having "inadvertently failed to list" an interest-free $15,000 loan made to his wife, Ursula. *March 14, 1984*

"I can control neither the inaccurate representation of my statements nor conclusions attributed to me by others. If my own statements, however, have offended you and Hispanic Americans, I apologize."

Philip Abrams, undersecretary of Housing and Urban Development, apologizing in a letter to the chairman of the Congressional Hispanics Caucus for opining to the *Washington Post* that overcrowded housing is "a characteristic of Hispanic communities, irrelevant to their social [and] economic conditions. It is a cultural preference, I'm told . . . I'm told they don't mind, and they prefer, some prefer, doubling up." *May 15, 1984*

"I'm sorry I carelessly gave the impression that I believed it had been totally eliminated in areas where it hasn't."

President Ronald Reagan apologizing for saying of South Africa, "They have eliminated the segregation that we once had in our own country—the type of thing where hotels and restaurants and places of entertainment and so forth were segregated—that has all been eliminated." *September 6, 1985*

"When I got back to the United States, I was actually horrified to find that that remark had been so misinterpreted. It was not intended as a put-down of any woman. And if anyone feels offended by it, I apologize."

White House chief of staff Donald Regan apologizing for observing that women would be more interested in stories about Nancy Reagan and Raisa Gorbachev than they would be in issue-oriented coverage of the Geneva summit. "They're not . . . going to understand throw weights or what is happening in Afghanistan or what is happening in human rights," he said. "Some women will, but most women . . . would rather read the human-interest stuff of what happened." *November 24, 1985*

——

"I wish I'd never said it because it's controversial and I have to explain and I'm very, very sorry about it."
Vice President George Bush apologizing in Brussels for offending U.S. auto workers by joking, after hearing about a Soviet military operation in which none of the 350 tanks involved broke down, "Hey, when the mechanics who keep those tanks running run out of work in the Soviet Union, send them to Detroit, because we could use that kind of ability." *October 3, 1987*

——

"Mrs. Mulligan, I'm calling you to apologize for the statement I made last week."
Vice President George Bush apologizing in a phone call to Kathleen Mulligan, a Boston mother of a Down's syndrome daughter, who was offended by his reference to rabid conservatives as "the extra-chromosome set." Bush explained that he thought he was using a political term and had no idea it referred to people with Down's syndrome. *December 16, 1987*

——

"I wouldn't have said what I said if I'd known the microphone was on. I would not have taken the Lord's name in vain, and I apologize for that because I was not amused, and I am afraid I said something that was not particularly appro-

priate. So I'd like to apologize for having said that. But please understand: You're looking at a competitor, and the adrenaline gets flowing. But I didn't know I was being taped either or I wouldn't have done that. You didn't hear me talk that way on the show."

Vice President George Bush apologizing for the intemperate remarks he made following a contentious live CBS interview with Dan Rather about his involvement in the Iran-Contra affair. "The bastard didn't lay a glove on me," Bush declared afterward, adding, "Tell your goddamned network that if they want to talk to me, to raise their hands at a press conference. No more Mr. Inside stuff after that." *January 27, 1988*

—

"I apologize not for the truth in my book nor the telling of it. The truth never requires apology. I do regret that I may have overstepped the bounds of propriety in some instances. It is for that I apologize."

Former White House spokesman Larry Speakes apologizing for passages in his book, *Speaking Out*, in which he revealed that in the midst of the 1983 Korean airliner crisis he credited words spoken by Secretary of State George Shultz to Ronald Reagan "since the President had had almost nothing to say." He also wrote that during the 1985 Geneva summit with Mikhail Gorbachev, he twice made up quotes and attributed them to Reagan, whose actual utterances had been "very tentative and stilted." *April 19, 1988*

—

"I regret any offense that may have been taken by an offhand comment made . . . in response to a reporter's question

about Danish elections. It was not meant to reflect on Denmark in any way."

White House press secretary Marlin Fitzwater apologizing for answering a reporter's question about an upcoming Danish ballot initiative by saying, "Danish means breakfast to me." *April 22, 1988*

—

"I apologize if I hurt anybody's feelings."

Mathew Panak, president of the Kinsman Township, OH, board of trustees, apologizing for scheduling a board meeting on Martin Luther King Jr. Day because "none of us is colored. It's not going to affect us. Nobody colored comes to the meetings anyway." Despite the apology, his true feelings continued to shine through when he told a reporter, "Reagan didn't get his. Kennedy got shot and he didn't get a holiday. They forgot all about the white people . . . We do enough for these people and they're still not happy. We gave them the right to vote and all that stuff." *January 13, 1995*

—

"There was never any intention to use this as an ethnic slur and we apologize to anyone who may be offended. The president simply used this word to point out that we must not fail deliberately to meet our obligations or debts."

White House spokeswoman Ginny Terzano apologizing for President Bill Clinton's statement, "The United States is a good citizen. We don't welsh on our debts." Said Rees Lloyd, lawyer for a Welsh American legal defense fund, "It's outrageous that the president of the United States would use this slur," though since the origin of the word has nothing whatsoever to do with the Welsh people, it actually wasn't a slur at all and the speedy apology was offered for a nonexistent offense. *September 22, 1995*

—

"I do not consider them evil, and I regret that my flip remark may have mistakenly created that impression."

Republican presidential candidate John McCain apologizing for referring to Pat Robertson and Rev. Jerry Falwell as "forces of evil." *March 1, 2000*

—

"It was a very poor choice of words and I apologize. I am very emotional on this subject because I feel we are very close to allowing the president to take an action that would result in hundreds of young American lives being lost."

Sen. James Inhofe (R-OK) apologizing for saying of President Bill Clinton's plan to send 25,000 peacekeeping troops into Bosnia, "This man, this idiot in the White House, has some deep-seated obsession with sending our young men and women into Bosnia when polls show most of the country is against the idea, and everybody knows hundreds of them will die." Inhofe exhibited no such indignance when George W. Bush sent hundreds of thousands of troops into Iraq, though he did come to the public's attention in the wake of the Abu Ghraib scandal by declaring himself "outraged" about the outrage of "humanitarian do-gooders . . . crawling all over these prisons, looking for human rights violations while our troops, our heroes, are fighting and dying." *October 31, 1995*

—

"The Corcoran Gallery of Art, in attempting to defuse the NEA funding controversy by removing itself from the political spotlight, has instead found itself in the center of controversy. By withdrawing from the Mapplethorpe exhibition, we, the board of trustees and the director, have inadvertently offended many members of the arts community, which we deeply regret. Our course in the future will be to support art, artists and freedom of artistic expression."

Washington, D.C.'s largest nonfederal museum in a statement apologizing for caving in to right-wing pressure and canceling Robert Mapplethorpe's exhibition of explicit sexual and homoerotic photographs, including his legendary self-portrait in leather with the handle of a bullwhip in his rectum. *September 19, 1989*

"I never saw it before the unveiling, and all I can say is that I apologize."

J. O. Stephenson, mayor of Little Kennesaw, GA, apologizing for the result of his town's rushing to be the first to name something after Gulf War hero H. Norman Schwarzkopf: a public ceremony at which the street sign honoring the general read "Schwartzkopf Court." *April 23, 1991*

"If any of my comments or actions have indeed been unwelcome or if I have conducted myself in any way that has caused any individual discomfort or embarrassment, for that I am sincerely sorry. My intentions were never to pressure, to offend, nor to make anyone feel uncomfortable, and I truly regret if that has occurred with anyone either on or off my staff."

Sen. Bob Packwood (R-OR) apologizing for anything he might have done that upset any of the ten women who had accused him of making unwanted sexual advances during his twenty-four years in Congress. Accusations against him included forcing kisses on women, chasing them around tables, and running his fingers through their hair. *November 22, 1992*

—

"This is clear. My past actions were not only inappropriate. What I did was not just stupid or boorish. My actions were just plain wrong . . . Although most of these incidents are a decade or two decades old, and no one's job or pay or status was threatened, my conduct was wrong. I just didn't get it. I do now. The important point is that my actions were unwelcome and insensitive. These women were offended, appropriately so, and I am truly sorry. It was not done with malice or evil intent. Now let me make these assurances. I plan to restructure, drastically and totally, my attitude and my professional relationships. If that requires professional counseling, I will seek it. I guarantee that nothing like this will ever happen again."

Sen. Bob Packwood apologizing again "for the conduct that it was alleged that I did" (while acknowledging no specific behavior) in an effort to quash demands that he resign, which he said he would not do "under any circumstances." *December 10, 1992*

—

"What I was apologizing for—and again, I want you to remember, Larry, at that time, the only charges were the seven that the *Washington Post* had brought up. And, of the seven, three women I didn't know. And none of the incidents did I recognize as they talked about them. So what I apologized for—and I'm paraphrasing it, because I can't remember [what] the exact words were—whatever it was I did, even if I couldn't remember it, I apologized for it. And I apologize for it again tonight. If I did things I can't remember, didn't know, or to people I didn't know, I'm embarrassed and I apologize. And that's what I meant."

Sen. Bob Packwood still apologizing, this time on CNN to Larry King. *March 30, 1994*

=

"Most of them are people I can't remember. I've apologized to the ones I can't remember, and I've apologized for the incidents I can't recall, and I apologize again."

Sen. Bob Packwood apologizing again to the nineteen women who claimed to have been on the receiving end of his unwanted sexual advances over a twenty-two-year period. Despite the Senate Ethics Committee investigation, though, he declared, "I have no intention of resigning now; not tomorrow, not next week, not next month, not next year." He resigned the next month after the committee recommended expulsion, which would have cost him his pension. *August 9, 1995*

=

"Am I sorry? Of course. If I did the things that they say I did, am I sorry, do I apologize? Yes. But it is time to get on and not look back."

Sen. Bob Packwood on CBS's *Face the Nation*, having announced his resignation. *September 10, 1995*

⎯

"My remarks were wrong, they were insensitive—although unintended in motivation—and unacceptable ... My regret is even more profound, I guess, because I believe my public record of thirty-two years as a congressman is without the slightest blot of racial insensitivity ... I ask that that lapse into insensitivity be measured against my public and private record and I have to apologize to all those who I've offended."

House Minority Leader Bob Michel (R-IL) apologizing for a TV interview in which he waxed nostalgic about minstrel shows ("Of course, today you can't do that—everybody black-faced up and 'Hey, Mr. Charlie, did you hear the one about ... ?' You know, I think it's too bad"), performed his "Amos 'n' Andy" impressions, and sang a bit of "Old Man River," bemoaning the fact that the original lyrics—which referred to blacks as "niggers"—had been revised ("Artistically and everything, I'd like to do it the way it was"). The gist of the interview? "It's too bad that ... we can't do some of the things that were part of our heritage." *November 16, 1988*

⎯

"I want to make it perfectly clear that I have no reason to think that the Audubon Society, the Sierra Club or any other conservation organization are in any way un-American. In fact, I believe to the contrary and I very much regret the confusion and the wrong implication that has come from it."

Assistant Secretary of Agriculture John Crowell apologizing for suggesting that environmental groups are often "infiltrated by people who have very strong ideas about socialism and even communism." *March 24, 1982*

———

**"I lost my cool, which I should not have done, and I apolo-
gize for that. But I actually apologize more to my friends and
my family for this kind of behavior which is caused by the
pressures placed on me because of my position."**

Michael Reagan apologizing for leaving a threatening
message on the answering machine of photographer Roger
Sandler, who was suing him for copyright infringement over
the use of two photos in his 1988 memoir, *On the Outside
Looking In.* Reagan's profane telephonic tirade ended, "I
hope your fucking family dies in a plane crash with you in
it." *January 24, 1989*

———

**"Call off the dogs please. I surrender. I apologize. I am chas-
tened and will never use 'hot tub' and 'Marin County' in the
same sentence again. I won't even try to explain my position
except to say I was and remain so offended by John Walker
Lindh that I hurt others' feelings."**

Former president George Bush apologizing for referring to
the American Taliban enlistee as a "poor misguided Marin
County hot-tubber." *February 27, 2002*

———

**"I want to express on behalf of the National Park Service our
deepest apology to the men and women of Los Alamos and
all of New Mexico."**

Bob Stanton, director of the National Park Service, apologizing for his agency's setting a fire (intended to control a
previously set underbrush-clearing fire that got out of
control) that got even more out of control than the first and

destroyed more than two hundred homes. Said Rep. Jay
Inslee (D-WA), "People do not pay their taxes for Uncle Sam
to burn down neighborhoods." *June 7, 2000*

═

**"I'd like to profoundly apologize to all and any I've offended
in any way either by name or by reference, because that was
not what I meant when I tried to be witty in my awkward
way."**

Virginia House delegate Vincent F. Callahan Jr. (R) apologizing for the latest version of his annual speech making fun
of his colleagues. Though this ritual had been silently
endured for years, his references to the menstrual cycle of
one delegate and his claim that female interns wore T-shirts
reading I WORKED ON THE SPEAKER'S STAFF finally prompted a
protest from Vivian Watts (D), who said before the session
that she should have complained last year after Callahan
joked about a male delegate who "wanted to jump-start" her.
Said Watts, "I'm a grandmother." *March 13, 1998*

═

**"I apologized to her for having embarrassed her and caused
her unhappiness. I told her very sincerely that I felt terrible
and hoped that she would accept my apology. This was an
incredibly dumb thing to do, incredibly dumb thing to say.
If I haven't learned a lesson, I deserve to be smacked on the
head by a two-by-four."**

Rep. Martin Hoke (R-OH) reporting his apology to Conus
Communications producer Lisa Dwyer, who was setting up
equipment for a video feed following President Bill Clinton's
State of the Union address when Hoke ogled her and,

unaware that his comment was being videotaped, told a colleague, "She has the *beeeg* breasts." *February 1, 1994*

———

"My comments were made in the spirit of the occasion. They may have been uncomfortable for you personally . . . It certainly was not my intention to offend or embarrass you. As you know from having attended these 'roasts' in the past, remarks are often freewheeling and, as evidenced by other roasters at the event, not always in good taste . . . If you personally took offense with what I said, I am truly sorry. Please accept my sincerest apology and assurances that I will not be on the giving end of a roast in the near future."

Prince George's County, MD, councilman Richard J. Castaldi apologizing to council chairwoman Hilda R. Pemberton for delivering remarks at her Democratic Party "roasting" that would have been better suited to a Friars Club roast of Whoopi Goldberg. "Now you can use your own imagination on how this is going to be used—I'm not going to go into details," he said at one point as he opened his "county councilwoman's date bag" and pulled out a box of plastic wrap. "But I have attached a real, live brochure from the well-respected Whitman-Walker Clinic on oral sex for women." (To truly convey the scope of the faux pas, it's worth noting that the oral sex clinic he referred to counseled AIDS patients, so on top of everything else, he could be seen as implying that she had AIDS.) There was also a short poem that he dedicated to her: "I'm tired of men who promise the moon, who keep going and coming—and always too soon." And Castaldi's breathtaking obtuseness continued unabated after the event, first by breezily telling the mortified and enraged fifty-three-year-old black woman "that I really was sorry if there was anything that was offensive"—IF!—and then by complaining that she was "blowing it out of proportion" by demanding a public apology. Said Gerard E. Evans, chairman of the local Democratic party of the otherwise enormously successful event, "I'd hate that this wonderful evening be remembered for an unfortunate incident." But, all these years later, of course it is. *September 23, 1993*

—

"I apologize to Gloria Allred and to all others who may have been wrongfully characterized, hurt or harmed in any way by these statements. I specifically apologize to Gloria Allred for any embarrassment or harm the release may have caused her . . . Based upon my past relationships with Gloria Allred, her husband and her family, I have never considered her to be and recognize that she is not a 'slick butch lawyeress.'"

Former congressman John Schmitz (R-CA), the father of convicted sex offender Mary Kay LeTourneau, apologizing in a written statement for calling Allred a "slick butch lawyeress" in a five-year-old press release, headlined SENATOR SCHMITZ AND HIS COMMITTEE SURVIVE "ATTACK OF THE BULLDYKES." The press release had also denounced Jews, women, and homosexuals ("pro-abortion queer groups"), all of whom also received a Schmitz apology. Allred also received twenty thousand dollars to settle a defamation suit. *August 21, 1986*

—

"I intended my remarks simply to be funny, but clearly it was inappropriate, a mistake, and I apologize. I've asked

everyone in my campaign to let those who were disturbed by my remarks know of my concern and my regret."

Democratic presidential candidate Bruce Babbitt apologizing for teasing fellow candidate Al Gore about his minimal campaign effort in the Iowa caucus by saying, "I thought they might start putting your picture on milk cartons," thereby offending the mother of a boy missing for more than five years whose picture had in fact appeared on milk cartons. *January 16, 1988*

"Conrad has teased his own daughter about her desire to get a nose ring in the past. But they compromised when she pierced the top of her ear. The comment was made in the same teasing spirit. But it obviously offended [Warren] and he's sorry for that and for anyone else who was offended. Conrad tells a lot of jokes. Not all of them are home runs."

Matt Raymond, spokesman for Sen. Conrad Burns (R-MT), apologizing for his boss's asking government worker Angela Warren, whose nose was pierced, "What is that thing in your nose? What tribe are you from?" Warren informed him, "It's a nose ring and I am obviously not from a tribe." *February 27, 2000*

"On behalf of President Clinton and the American people, I wish to apologize."

U.S. ambassador Thomas Foglietta apologizing for the recklessness of the crew of a Marine fighter jet who, by flying too fast and too low through the Italian Alps, managed to sever two ski lift cables and send twenty people plunging to their deaths. *March 12, 1998*

—

"It wasn't done purposely. I do apologize to all my friends in the United States and here that I didn't mention this. If I misled them, I'm sorry."

Austrian presidential candidate and former United Nations secretary general Kurt Waldheim apologizing on *60 Minutes* for not revealing that he'd been in the German Army from 1942 to 1945, though he pointed out that, as a mere desk officer, he gave no orders and knew nothing of atrocities. *April 13, 1986*

—

"I made a serious mistake. I should have not been in the company of any woman not my wife who was not a friend of mine or my wife . . . I should not have been with Miss Rice."

Sen. Gary Hart (D-CO) apologizing on ABC's *Nightline* for his error in having spent the night in his Washington home with model Donna Rice, who—judging from photos of her sitting in his lap—certainly seemed to be a friend of his, if not of his wife's. Lesson: if you're widely believed to be a womanizer, don't issue a challenge like this to the press: "Follow me around. I don't care. I'm serious. If anybody wants to put a tail on me, go ahead. They'd be very bored." *September 7, 1987*

—

"I'm sorry that I made a mistake. It happened three years ago. I'm human, and in no way did I violate my oath of office. I only hope my wife and children will forgive me."

Rep. Daniel Crane (R-IL) apologizing for having sex several times with a seventeen-year-old female page. *July 14, 1983*

—

"That was a very intemperate remark made in the heat of the day yesterday in a very misguided attempt to defend my boss. I'm very sorry for it and I apologize to Congress for it. It in no way reflects my feelings or opinions of Congress."

Rep. Daniel Crane's press secretary, William Mencarow, apologizing for telling reporters, "If they required the resignation of all congressmen who have slept with young ladies, you wouldn't have a Congress." *July 15, 1983*

"If anybody's been offended, I'm pleased to apologize to them. I don't want to offend people. That's not my intention nor is it the intention of my family."

Gov. John Ashcroft (R-MO) apologizing for his wife Janet's intruding on state librarian Monteria Hightower's Mother's Day celebration by having her come and open the state library on a Sunday night so Mrs. Ashcroft could help her son with a homework assignment. "I assume that every parent knows that there are times when their kid isn't as prepared as he ought to be for school," the governor said, "and what you do is you help 'em." *May 18, 1990*

"I made statements that created the wrong impression about the Hispanic community and want to just deeply apologize to those I've offended."

Texas health commissioner William "Reyn" Archer apologizing for blaming the state's high teen-pregnancy rate on its Hispanic population's perception of pregnancy as "a positive thing." As he explained to a reporter, "Society values pregnancies in teenagers as bad, but certain communities within society may feel differently." Said Rep. Charlie Gonzalez (D-TX), "I don't know why people would be so impressed with an apology for something that is so blatantly offensive." *April 18, 2000*

———

"It was a mistake. People were asking me questions at the time and I responded, but nobody knows better than I the pain that can be caused by ever discussing rumors in private conversation."

Hillary Clinton apologizing for complaining to *Vanity Fair* writer Gail Sheehy about the press's double standard evidenced by its obsession with her husband's private life and its apparent indifference to "Bush and his carrying on, all of which is apparently well known in Washington." *April 4, 1992*

———

"I apologize to the African-American community and to all people for saying that Dr. Martin Luther King Jr. was a great man for the black people alone. He was a great American for all Americans. The celebration of Dr. King's birthday does not depend on the number of blacks in a community. It is a holiday which is celebrated by everyone who believes in brotherhood and justice, and the Village of Bradley recognizes that."

Bradley, IL, mayor Kenneth Hayes apologizing for his reaction to the idea of making King's birthday a paid holiday: "Martin Luther King was a great man for the black people ... We have five or six blacks in Bradley. Why should we close down services for the other 11,995?" *December 12, 1990*

———

"I just wanted to say that a lot of the stuff I put out was wrong and it was hateful. And you can call that a retraction . . . I never imagined that my words were going to be the focus of such intense media scrutiny. But I really don't have anyone to blame for that but myself."

Recently elected and newly resigned New Hampshire state legislator Tom Alciere apologizing for his relentless advocacy—in hundreds of Internet postings discovered only after this Libertarian former Wal-Mart night-shift maintenance man took office—of killing police officers. Among his postings, which he took pains to keep from voters during his stealth campaign as a Republican: "The only thing that ever gets through a cop's head is a bullet," "Nobody will ever be safe until the last cop is dead," and "Speak highly of the cop-killers, for they are America's only hope." As recently as the day before this apology was brought forth, he'd been on the radio pointing out that anyone so inclined would do well to consider the "opportunities" provided by construction sites, where cops on the premises could easily be mowed down by supposedly out-of-control vehicles. *January 12, 2001*

"I did not mean to suggest that Gov. Wilson is anti-Semitic. He clearly is not. I misspoke. The words I used yesterday were a total mistake."

California lieutenant governor (and future governor, and future recalled governor) Gray Davis apologizing on the campaign trail for saying, "Wilson likes to fan the flames of discontent, anti-Semitism and bigotry." History records no reporter asking him to speculate as to why someone who isn't anti-Semitic enjoys fanning anti-Semitic flames. *June 1, 1998*

———

"It never occurred to me that they would be offended and if I offended anybody in any way I certainly apologize."

Texas businessman and independent presidential candidate H. Ross Perot apologizing for addressing blacks at a Nashville NAACP convention as "you people." *July 11, 1992*

———

"Our reputation has been tarnished. We have no business being engaged in this kind of activity, and I am sorry it happened . . . The damage done to the governor, if there has been any, I apologize for it. More fundamentally, I apologize for the department being in this mess."

Acting Secretary of State Lawrence S. Eagleburger apologizing for the State Department's search of Bill Clinton's passport files in the hope of finding something to be used against him in the presidential campaign. *November 18, 1992*

———

"I am sorry for exercising bad judgment and can assure everyone this will never happen again."

Columba Bush, wife of Florida governor Jeb, apologizing for failing to declare $19,000 in clothing and jewelry purchased in Paris to customs officials in Atlanta. The $4,100 fine she paid was triple what she would have paid had she simply been honest in the first place. *June 18, 1999*

———

"Although the vast majority of the material was completely accurate, some mistakes and omissions were made. I take responsibility for those mistakes . . . I want to apologize to you if this matter has caused you any embarrassment . . . I am sickened by the thought that anyone would think that I would purposefully release anything less than completely accurate information."

Rep. Dan Burton (R-IN), who had recently told a reporter that he was "out to get" President Bill Clinton because he's a "scumbag," apologizing to his colleagues for releasing selected portions of taped prison conversations between long-time Clinton friend Webster Hubbell and his wife that curiously failed to include any of several exculpatory comments about the Clintons. *June 6, 1998*

⸻

"I have apologized to my wife and family, whom I love. I apologize to my constituents. We live in a society that rightfully depends upon people taking responsibility for their actions. I have done so in this matter."

Rep. Dan Burton (R-IN) acknowledging that he had a teenage son from an extramarital relationship. *September 4, 1998*

⸻

"Today I rise on a point of personal privilege to publicly apologize to my constituents, to each and every member of this body, to the staff of the Senate and, in particular, to our impressionable young pages and messengers for any embarrassment occasioned by my recent actions."

State senator Thomas K. Norment Jr. (R-VA), who'd been quite vocal about the need to get tough with drunk drivers, apologizing after his arrest for guess what. *January 24, 2001*

⸻

"I am extremely mortified at a mix-up in words in my prior remarks . . . I also want to apologize to my colleagues for this unfortunate and insensitive mistake."

Sen. Orrin Hatch (R-UT), whose unlikely friendship with Sen. Ted Kennedy (D-MA) is one of the mysteries of the Senate, apologizing for embarrassing his friend when, while defending Sen. Arlen Specter (R-PA) against Kennedy's attacks on his shameful behavior in the Clarence Thomas hearings, he blurted out an odd twist on a familiar phrase: "If you believe that, I've got a bridge in Massachusetts that I'll sell you." Hatch, who perhaps had been subliminally sabotaged by the Chappaquiddick signs carried by pro-Thomas demonstrators, requested that the written record replace "Massachusetts" with "Brooklyn." *October 15, 1991*

⸺

"I am painfully aware that the criticism directed at me in recent months involves far more than honest disagreements with my positions, or the usual criticism from the far right. It also involves the disappointment of friends and many others who rely on me to fight the good fight. To them I say: I recognize my own shortcomings—the faults in the conduct of my private life. I realize that I alone am responsible for them, and I am the one who must confront them. I believe that each of us as individuals must not only struggle to make a better world, but to make ourselves better, too."

Sen. Ted Kennedy apologizing for allowing the endless personal scandals—most recently his carousing with nephew William hours before said nephew had a sexual encounter that ended with a rape charge—to blunt his effectiveness as a champion of women's issues. *October 25, 1991*

—

"I do not recall making the racial slur comment. If I did make this statement, it was a slip of the tongue and I am very sorry of it."

Fremont, NE, city councilman Gerald Row apologizing for using this argument against putting group homes for the mentally retarded in his district: "It would be like a black family moving in next door. You wouldn't want that. And your property value would drop." *January 30, 1986*

—

"We came too early to the White House feed and then had technical difficulties getting our studio shot back. We are very sorry, have apologised and will not be using that footage again."

The BBC apologizing for its accidental live broadcast—to hundreds of millions of viewers in some two hundred countries—of George W. Bush with his eyes darting impishly back and forth as his hair and makeup were being tweaked just before his TV speech announcing that the invasion of Iraq had begun. *March 20, 2003*

—

"I called Rove and apologized for what I said."

Senate Minority Leader Harry Reid (D-NV) reporting that he called the White House and apologized to adviser Karl Rove for saying of George W. Bush, "The man's father is a wonderful human being. I think this guy is a loser." *May 6, 2005*

—

"Your government failed you. Those entrusted with protecting you failed you. And I failed you. We tried hard. But that doesn't matter, because we failed. And for that failure, I would ask, once all the facts are out, for your understanding and for your forgiveness."

Former counterterrorism chief Richard A. Clarke apologizing to the families of the 9/11 victims for his inability to instill any sense of urgency in George W. Bush or his minions about CIA memos with headlines like BIN LADEN DETERMINED TO STRIKE IN U.S. *March 24, 2004*

—

"I mistakenly suggested that increasing violence in the Middle East was attributable to the peace efforts that were underway in 2000. That is not the position of the administration . . . No United States president, including President Clinton, is to blame for violence in the Middle East. The only people to blame for violence are the terrorists who engage in it. I regret any implication to the contrary."

White House spokesman Ari Fleischer apologizing for blaming Middle East violence on Bill Clinton. *February 28, 2002*

—

"My criticisms were groundless and baseless due to poorly chosen words and examples. I sincerely apologize and I am deeply remorseful."

John DiIulio, former director of George W. Bush's faith-based initiative, apologizing (using language that echoed White House spokesman Ari Fleischer's attack on him) for telling *Esquire* reporter Ron Suskind, "There is no precedent in any modern

White House for what is going on in this one: a complete lack of a policy apparatus. What you've got is everything, and I mean everything, being run by the political arm. It's the reign of the Mayberry Machiavellis." *December 2, 2002*

"I remember when Winston Churchill once said that he frequently had to eat his words and in general he found it a wholesome diet. I regret that my comments were misconstrued."

Budget director Mitchell E. Daniels Jr., who infuriated New York lawmakers by saying that five billion dollars in victim compensation would count as part of the twenty billion dollars pledged to the city by George W. Bush for post-9/11 recovery costs, apologizing for infuriating them further by describing their criticism of this plan as "a little money-grubbing game." *February 4, 2002*

"I can't tell you how sorry I am to them and their families for the humiliation. I'm also sorry because people are then able to say, 'Look how terrible America is.'"

George W. Bush apologizing to Egyptian newspaper *al-Ahram* for Abu Ghraib. *May 6, 2004*

"If Nicole and Jeff Rank did nothing other than peaceably exercise their right of free speech and expression as guaranteed by our Constitutions, they should not have been arrested or charged with a crime. The City does hereby apologize to Nicole and Jeff Rank."

The Charleston, WV, City Council apologizing in a resolution to a pair of protesters who were handcuffed and arrested for trespassing after showing up at George W. Bush's July 4 rally wearing LOVE AMERICA, HATE BUSH T-shirts. *July 19, 2004*

⸻

"I fully understand people's disgust at what I wrote. It is something that I wish I had never done and indeed find it difficult to believe that I did. It is something I will have to live with for the rest of my life."

Jo Moore, adviser to Britain's transport secretary, apologizing for the "terrible error in judgment" that prompted her to send out this e-mail following the collapse of the World Trade Center towers: "It is now a very good day to get out anything we want to bury." *October 16, 2001*

⸻

"I should have disclosed a government contract when I later wrote about the Bush marriage initiative. I would have, if I had remembered it. My apologies to my readers."

Syndicated columnist Maggie Gallagher apologizing for managing to forget to mention that in 2002, when she was writing column after column in support of George W. Bush's "marriage initiative," she'd received $21,500 from the Department of Health and Human Services to help promote that very initiative. *January 25, 2005*

⸻

"It was prideful and arrogant of me to think my good intentions justified my actions . . . I was foolish and wrong to tape-record Mr. Bush without his permission. I was wrong to play

any part of the tapes for my publisher, regardless of the circumstances. I was wrong to play any part of them for a journalist . . . The hours of tapes, which prompted offers of millions of dollars, have been turned over to the president."

Doug Wead, friend of George W. Bush, in an article he wrote for *USA Today* headlined I'M SORRY, MR. PRESIDENT, apologizing not only for secretly taping conversations with George W. Bush but also for using their contents in his book *The Raising of a President* to address some of Bush's least favorite subjects—his never-actually-denied past marijuana and cocaine use and his fears about their impact on his presidential campaign. *March 14, 2005*

—

"Charlie Brooker apologises for any offence caused by his comments relating to President Bush in his TV column, Screen Burn. The views expressed in this column are not those of the *Guardian*. Although flippant and tasteless, his closing comments were intended as an ironic joke, not as a call to action—an intention he believed regular readers of his humorous column would understand. He deplores violence of any kind."

The [U.K.] *Guardian* apologizing for columnist Charlie Brooker's screed attacking George W. Bush as "a lying, sniggering, drink-driving, selfish, reckless, ignorant, dangerous, backward, drooling, twitching, blinking, mouse-faced little cheat" and asking, "John Wilkes Booth, Lee Harvey Oswald, John Hinckley Jr.—where are you now that we need you?" *October 25, 2004*

"I apologize. I made a dumb mistake. I'm sorry. I'm paying a big price for that mistake."

Rep. Donald "Buz" Lukens (R-OH), with his mother present, apologizing for his conviction on the charge of having sex with a sixteen-year-old girl as he announced his reelection campaign. He was defeated in the primary a week later. *May 2, 1990*

"While my comment was made in jest, it could be misunderstood by those who were not in attendance. I recognize that my comment could offend and I apologize to anyone who may have been offended."

Gov. Frank Keating (R-OK) apologizing for replying, when asked what was the best method for dealing with his state's teachers' union, "Homicide." *February 3, 2000*

"I regret that in the heat of the moment I spoke unwisely. I meant to express that at a time when we have a shortage of jobs, a lack of adequate health care, a problem with adequately educating our people and an administration entirely opposed and unsympathetic to these needs, we cannot afford to take on more."

Sen. Robert Byrd (D-WV) apologizing for a rant that seemed to suggest that the United States should stop admitting non-English-speaking immigrants: "I pick up the telephone and call the local garage. I can't understand the person on the other side of the line. I'm not sure he can understand me. They're all over the place, and they don't speak English. Do we want more of this?" *June 26, 1992*

"That party got out of hand, and there were some activities on stage that many people found shocking. We ask our friends, and my foes, to stay focused on what this campaign is really about—10,000 jobs, a new stadium and keeping the 49ers in San Francisco."

Political consultant Jack Davis, manager of the effort to get the city to build a new football stadium, apologizing to the team and to "all of those in attendance [at my fiftieth-birthday party] who took offense" at things like a three-hundred-plus-pound man performing oral sex on his partner and a leather-clad dominatrix who carved a satanic star into a man's back, urinated on him, and sodomized him with a Jack Daniels bottle. *May 8, 1997*

—

"Obviously some mistakes were made. Certainly I regret that my own mistakes contributed to this controversy."

Chief of staff John H. Sununu apologizing for creating the "appearance of impropriety" with his disregard of the rules regulating use by White House staffers of corporate aircraft, along with his use of government jets and limos for nonofficial business (i.e., being driven from Washington, D.C. to New York for a stamp auction). *June 22, 1991*

—

"I deeply regret that I did not correct the statement before this time. I truly ask your forgiveness."

State representative Robert C. Sorensen (D-CT) apologizing for falsely claiming during a rancorous debate about the Pledge of Allegiance, "My patriotism should not be questioned by anyone because when it was necessary and when my country called me into service, I fought in Vietnam." Sorensen explained that due to the ubiquitousness of the war on television, "every single person in the United States fought that war in Vietnam. We were all a part of that war. There was a part of all of us there. So, in a sense, I was there." *September 18, 1984*

<hr>

"I deeply regret and apologize for my wrong choice of words in a recent opinion survey which I thought was confidential. I was wrong in what I said."

State representative Russell J. Reynolds (D-CT) apologizing for responding to a query about state taxes on a United Press International questionnaire by writing, "No! No! No income tax. No more taxes. Limit spending. Put the niggers back to work." Censured days later by the state House of Representatives, Reynolds said, "I stand as one who has brought shame upon myself and this Assembly. No excuse is acceptable and none can be offered." And no explanation of what it was about a questionnaire from UPI that suggested confidentiality to him. *February 15, 1980*

<hr>

"Sometimes I get a little more passionate, and particularly during the moment and the day that Terri Schiavo was starved to death, emotions were flowing. I said something in an inartful way and I shouldn't have said it that way and I apologize for saying it that way. It was taken wrong. I didn't explain it or clarify my remarks, as I'm clarifying them here. I am sorry that I said it that way, and I shouldn't have."

House Majority Leader Tom DeLay (R-TX) apologizing for seeming to threaten retaliation against the federal judges who refused to reinstate brain-damaged Terri Schiavo's feeding tube when, railing against an "arrogant, out-of-control, unaccountable judiciary," he said ominously, "The time will come for the men responsible for this to answer for their behavior." *April 13, 2005*

"I am very, very sorry that anybody in my campaign in any way contributed to what was a very, very painful experience for [Joe Biden] and for his family and his supporters."

Massachusetts governor and Democratic presidential primary candidate Michael Dukakis apologizing for his aide John Sasso's distribution of the so-called attack video showing that rival candidate Sen. Joe Biden lifted several passages from a speech by British Labour Party leader Neil Kinnock without crediting him. Since Biden actually did do this, Dukakis was basically apologizing—and apologizing and apologizing, as the groveling contrition went on for days— for telling the truth. *October 2, 1987*

"In 1988, fighting Dukakis, I said that I 'would strip the bark off the little bastard' and 'make Willie Horton his running mate.' I am sorry for both statements: the first for its naked cruelty, the second because it makes me sound racist, which I am not."

Republican Party chairman Lee Atwater, suffering from an inoperable brain tumor, apologizing for the brutal campaign tactics he'd championed back when he felt invulnerable. *January 12, 1991*

"I understand some people were offended by my remarks and to those individuals I apologize. Arab Americans deserve the same degree of respect and dignity afforded to other groups in northern Michigan, the Upper Peninsula and anywhere else for that matter. There is no room in the 1990s for maliciously smearing someone's ethnicity."

Rep. Bob Davis (R-MI) apologizing for telling crude jokes about Iraqi women at the annual Upper Peninsula Legislative Dinner. Among them: "What is the difference between a catfish and an Iraqi woman? One has whiskers and smells bad, and the other is a fish." Said his press secretary, "It's a safe assumption he will not be telling jokes like this in the future." *March 27, 1991*

"Like most Arizonans, I have tried to determine why our state is now so politically divided. I have come to the conclusion that some, but not all, of the blame rests with me. I apologize to the people of Arizona for any of my actions or mistakes which may have sparked embarrassing publicity for our state. I have been well intentioned but I now know that I may have been the cause of legitimate concern. I hope the people of our great state will balance these errors against the good things which I have done, accept my apology and forgive me for my mistakes."

Governor Evan Mecham (R) on the eve of the start of impeachment proceedings against him and with a recall drive well underway, apologizing in a letter to the *Arizona Republic* for anything he needs to apologize for. Among his offenses: indictment on felony perjury and fraud charges, and disallowing pay for state workers on Martin Luther King

Jr.'s birthday, which led to the cancellation of several conventions to have been held in the state. He was soon impeached and removed from office. *January 15, 1988*

—

"This is a good time to say I'm sorry. When I called him 'Pruneface,' it was campaign rhetoric."

Detroit mayor Coleman Young (D) apologizing for repeatedly referring to Ronald Reagan as "Pruneface from the west" and, after his election, as "President Pruneface." *December 17, 1980*

—

"This was a lighthearted celebration of the 100th birthday of legendary Senator Strom Thurmond. My comments were not an endorsement of his positions of over fifty years ago, but of the man and his life."

Senate Republican leader Trent Lott of Mississippi, not yet apologizing for this gust of political flatulence: "I want to say this about my state. When Strom Thurmond ran for president [in 1948 as the segregationist Dixiecrat candidate], we voted for him. We're proud of it. And if the rest of the country had followed our lead, we wouldn't have had all these problems over all these years either." *December 9, 2002*

—

"A poor choice of words conveyed to some the impression that I embraced the discarded policies of the past. Nothing could be further from the truth, and I apologize to anyone who was offended by my statement."

Trent Lott, his innocent longing for a segregationist in the

White House fifty-plus years ago having been poorly received, delivering his first official apology even as he remained blissfully unaware that he had embarked on a weeklong parade of penance. *December 9, 2002*

⸺

"My comments conveyed things I do not intend, and I regret and, you know, I apologize for it."
Trent Lott with Apology II, this time to Fox News conservative Sean Hannity, for his "mistake of the head—and not the heart" at the Thurmond bash. "The words were terrible, and I regret this," he acknowledged, explaining that when he said we'd have been better off with Thurmond, he wasn't approving of the man's racism. No, it was his support for "a strong national defense and economic development and balanced budgets and opportunity" that so appealed to Lott. *December 11, 2002*

⸺

"Look, you put your foot in your mouth, you're getting carried away at a ceremony honoring a guy like this, you go too far. Those words were insensitive, and I shouldn't have said them . . . I regret it and I apologize for it."
Trent Lott delivering Apology III on CNN to Larry King. *December 11, 2002*

⸺

"Senator Lott agrees with President Bush that his words were wrong and he is sorry. He repudiates segregation because it is immoral."
Trent Lott responding to George W. Bush's throwing him

overboard by saying that his comments "do not reflect the spirit of our country" in Apology IV. *December 12, 2002*

"Segregation is a stain on our nation's soul. There's no other way to describe it. It represents one of the lowest moments in our nation's history, and we can never forget that . . . Let me be clear. Segregation and racism are immoral . . . I've asked and I'm asking for forbearance and forgiveness as I continue to learn from my own mistakes and as I continue to grow and get older . . . I apologize for opening old wounds and hurting many Americans who feel so deeply in this area. I take full responsibility for my remarks. I can't say it was prepared remarks. As a matter of fact, I was winging it. I was too much into the moment. But I only hope that people will find it in their heart to forgive me for that grievous mistake on that occasion."

Trent Lott offering Apology V at a press conference in his hometown of Pascagoula, where he defended his abysmal Senate voting record by pointing out that though he voted against the Martin Luther King holiday (which even Thurmond voted for), "I did vote to put a bust [of King] in the Capitol because there was a lot of support for it, and I thought that that was something that would help bring about reconciliation." *December 13, 2002*

"I accept the fact that I made a terrible mistake, used horrible words, caused hurt. I'm sorry about that. I apologize for it. I've asked for forgiveness and I'm going to continue to do that . . . But it is about actions more than

words. As majority leader I can move an agenda that would hopefully be helpful to African Americans and minorities of all kinds and all Americans."

Trent Lott, dubbed by columnist George Will "the serial apologizer," offering Apology VI during a thirty-minute grovel on Black Entertainment Television, where he told interviewer Ed Gordon, "To be a racist, you have to feel superior. I don't feel superior to you at all." His big announcement: he now supports the King holiday (as *Milwaukee Journal Sentinel* columnist Eugene Kane wrote, "Heck, we don't need you now! We already have the King holiday, fool!"). Oh, and, "I'm for affirmative action and I've practiced it. I've had African Americans on my staff and other minorities, but particularly African Americans, since the mid-1970s." The general consensus after a full week of contrition was that Lott was at best insensitive and at worst an unreconstructed racist who carelessly spoke his mind and then had to humiliate himself in an effort to hold on to his power position as Senate party leader—an effort that officially failed four days after the BET appearance when he resigned his leadership position. In any event, with his groveling Apol-Orgy of six distinct efforts in eight days, Trent Lott is the twenty-first century's reigning king of contrition, the ayatollah of atonement, the rajah of regret. *December 16, 2002*

—

"As you know, in a deposition in January I was asked questions about my relationship with Monica Lewinsky. While my answers were legally accurate, I did not volunteer information. Indeed, I did have a relationship with Miss Lewinsky that was not appropriate. In fact, it was wrong. It

constituted a critical lapse in judgment and a personal failure on my part, for which I am solely and completely responsible . . . I know that my public comments and my silence about this matter gave a false impression. I misled people, including even my wife. I deeply regret that."

President Bill Clinton acknowledging a certain lack of forthrightness in his earlier handling of *l'affaire* Lewinsky. *August 17, 1998*

"I agree with those who have said that, in my first statement after I testified, I was not contrite enough. I don't think there is a fancy way to say that I have sinned. It is important to me that everybody who has been hurt know that the sorrow I feel is genuine—first and most important, my family, also my friends, my staff, my cabinet, Monica Lewinsky and her family, and the American people. I have asked all for their forgiveness.

"But I believe that to be forgiven, more than sorrow is required. At least two more things: First, genuine repentance, a determination to change and to repair breaches of my own making. I have repented. Second, what my Bible calls a broken spirit. An understanding that I must have God's help to be the person that I want to be. A willingness to give the very forgiveness I seek. A renunciation of the pride and the anger, which cloud judgment, lead people to excuse and compare and to blame and complain . . .

"And if my repentance is genuine and sustained, and if I can then maintain both a broken spirit and a strong heart, then good can come of this for our country, as well as for me and my family. The children of this country can learn in a profound way that integrity is important and selfishness is wrong. But God can change us and make us strong at the broken places. I want to embody those lessons for the children of this country . . .

"A couple of days ago when I was in Florida, a Jewish friend of mine gave me this liturgy book called *Gates of Repentance*. And there was this incredible passage from a Yom Kippur liturgy, and I would like to read it to you: 'Now is the time for turning. The leaves are beginning to turn from green to red to orange. The birds are beginning to turn and are heading once more toward the south. The animals are beginning to turn to storing their food for the winter. For leaves, birds, and animals, turning comes instinctively. But for us, turning does not come so easily. It takes an act of will for us to make a turn. It means breaking old habits. It means admitting that we have been wrong, and this is never easy. It means losing face. It means starting all over again. And this is always painful. It means saying I am sorry. It means recognizing that we have the ability to change. These things are terribly hard to do. But unless we turn, we will be trapped forever in yesterday's ways. Lord help us to turn from callousness to sensitivity, from hostility to love, from pettiness to purpose, from envy to contentment, from carelessness to discipline, from fear to faith. Turn us around, O Lord, and bring us back toward you. Revive our lives as at the beginning. And turn us toward each other, Lord, for in isolation, there is no life.'

"I thank my friend for that and I thank you for being here. I ask you to share my prayer that God will search me and know my heart, try me and know my anxious thoughts, see if there is any hurtfulness in me and lead me toward a life everlasting. I ask that God give me a clean heart, let me walk by faith and not sight. I ask once again to be able to love my neighbor—all my neighbors—as myself, to be an instrument of God's peace, to let the words of my mouth and the meditations of my heart, and in the end, the work of my hands, be pleasing.

"This is what I wanted to say to you today. Thank you, God bless you."

President Bill Clinton at a White House prayer breakfast. Love him or hate him, folks, *that*'s an apology. *September 11, 1998*

Future Imperfect

For the apologies of offenders who have come forward after this book was set in type—among them Washington lobbyist Jack Abramoff for tax evasion, fraud, and bribery; Rep. Randy "Duke" Cunningham (R-CA) for bribe taking; White House shill Bob Woodward for overprotecting his Bush administration sources; Pat Robertson for suggesting that God punished Ariel Sharon with a stroke because he gave land to the Palestinians; New Orleans mayor C. Ray Nagin for saying Hurricane Katrina was a sign that God was "mad at America"; skier Bode Miller for boasting that he raced drunk; and Rep. Jean Schmidt (R-OH) for calling Rep. John Murtha (D-PA), a decorated marine, a "coward" for supporting the pullout of U.S. forces from Iraq—please visit the *My Bad* Web site at www.vidlit.com/mybad.

Index

A Note on the Authors

Paul Slansky is the author of *The Clothes Have No Emperor* and *The George W. Bush Quiz Book*. His work is frequently featured in the *New Yorker*.

Arleen Sorkin is a film and television writer, producer, and actress. She is coproducer of the play *RFK*.